The Economics of
Macro Issues

D0145480

The Pearson Series in Economics

Abel/Bernanke/Croushore
*Macroeconomics**
Bade/Parkin
*Foundations of Economics**
Berck/Helfand
The Economics of the Environment
Bierman/Fernandez
Game Theory with Economic Applications
Blanchard
*Macroeconomics**
Blau/Ferber/Winkler
The Economics of Women, Men and Work
Boardman/Greenberg/Vining/ Weimer
Cost-Benefit Analysis
Boyer
Principles of Transportation Economics
Branson
Macroeconomic Theory and Policy
Brock/Adams
The Structure of American Industry
Bruce
Public Finance and the American Economy
Carlton/Perloff
Modern Industrial Organization
Case/Fair/Oster
*Principles of Economics**
Caves/Frankel/Jones
World Trade and Payments: An Introduction
Chapman
Environmental Economics: Theory, Application, and Policy
Cooter/Ulen
Law & Economics
Downs
An Economic Theory of Democracy

Ehrenberg/Smith
Modern Labor Economics
Farnham
Economics for Managers
Folland/Goodman/Stano
The Economics of Health and Health Care
Fort
Sports Economics
Froyen
Macroeconomics
Fusfeld
The Age of the Economist
Gerber
*International Economics**
González-Rivera
Forecasting for Economics and Business
Gordon
*Macroeconomics**
Greene
Econometric Analysis
Gregory
Essentials of Economics
Gregory/Stuart
Russian and Soviet Economic Performance and Structure
Hartwick/Olewiler
The Economics of Natural Resource Use
Heilbroner/Milberg
The Making of the Economic Society
Heyne/Boettke/Prychitko
The Economic Way of Thinking
Hoffman/Averett
Women and the Economy: Family, Work, and Pay
Holt
Markets, Games and Strategic Behavior
Hubbard/O'Brien
*Economics**
*Money, Banking, and the Financial System**

*denotes MyEconLab titles.   Visit **www.myeconlab.com** to learn more.

The Economics of
Macro Issues

SIXTH EDITION

Roger LeRoy Miller
Research Professor of Economics
University of Texas–Arlington

Daniel K. Benjamin
Clemson University, South Carolina
and PERC, Bozeman, Montana

Boston Columbus Indianapolis New York San Francisco Upper Saddle River
Amsterdam Cape Town Dubai London Madrid Milan Munich Paris MontrealToronto
Delhi Mexico City Sao Paulo Sydney Hong Kong Seoul Singapore Taipei Tokyo

Editor in Chief: Donna Battista
Executive Editor: David Alexander
Sr. Editorial Project Manager: Carolyn Terbush
Editorial Assistant: Patrick Henning
Director of Marketing: Maggie Moylan
Marketing Manager: Lori DeShazo
Marketing Assistant: Kim Lovato
Managing Editor: Jeff Holcomb
Sr. Production Project Manager:
  Kathryn Dinovo

Sr. Manufacturing Buyer: Carol Melville
Art Director: Jayne Conte
Cover Art: Fotolia
Full-Service Project Management: Cenveo®
  Publisher Services/Nesbitt Graphics
Printer/Binder: Edwards Brothers Malloy
  Jackson Road
Cover Printer: Lehigh-Phoenix
  Color/Hagerstown
Text Font: Times LT Std

Credits and acknowledgments borrowed from other sources and reproduced, with permission, in this textbook appear on the appropriate page within text.

Library of Congress Cataloging-in-Publication Data
Miller, Roger LeRoy.
The economics of macro issues / Roger LeRoy Miller, Research Professor of Economics University of Texas, Arlington, Daniel K. Benjamin, Clemson University, South Carolina and PERC, Bozeman, Montana. —Sixth Edition.
    pages cm. —(The Pearson series in economics)
Includes bibliographical references and index.
ISBN 978-0-13-299128-5
1. Macroeconomics.   I. Benjamin, Daniel K.   II. Title.
HB172.5.M53 2013
339—dc23

                                                            2013019029

10 9 8 7 6 5 4

ISBN-10: 0-13-299128-4
ISBN-13: 978-0-13-299128-5

To Simon,
Keep pushing me to go faster.
—R.L.M.

To Bryan and Tucker,
Senior members of the crew.
—D.K.B.

CONTENTS

PART THREE
Fiscal Policy   77

PART FOUR
Monetary Policy and Financial Institutions   123

SUGGESTIONS FOR USE

At the request of our readers, we include the following table to help you incorporate the chapters of this book into your syllabus. Depending on the breadth of your course, you may also want to consult the companion paperback, *The Economics of Public Issues,* 18th edition, which features microeconomics topics and a similar table in its preface.

Economics Topics	Recommended Chapters in The Economics of Macro Issues, 6th Edition
Taxes and Public Spending	4, 7, 10, 12, 17
Unemployment, Inflation, and Deflation	7, 8, 10, 11, 20
Measuring the Economy's Performance	5, 6
Economic Growth and Development	1, 2, 3, 4, 5, 13
Classical and Keynesian Macro Analyses	6, 7, 9, 13, 18
Fiscal Policy	12, 13, 14, 15, 16, 17, 18
Deficits and the Public Debt	10, 12, 13, 14, 15, 16, 17, 18
Money and Banking	10, 19, 20, 22, 23
Money Creation and Deposit Insurance	19, 20, 21, 22
Monetary Policy: Domestic and International	20, 23, 24, 25, 27
Stabilization and the Global Economy	24, 25, 26
International Trade	1, 2, 3, 24, 25, 26
International Finance	24, 25
Recession	5, 6, 7, 8, 9, 13, 14, 15

PREFACE

Times have changed, and so has this book. The macroeconomic policy scene has continued to evolve rapidly over a remarkably short period of time. Since our last revision, the United States has struggled to recover from one of the most severe recessions of the past hundred years, and both fiscal and monetary policies have moved to play an even greater role in the economy. Federal spending and the deficit have exploded. Agencies of the U.S. government—ranging from the Treasury to government-sponsored enterprises—are now the *de facto* guarantors of most of the U.S. housing market and virtually every large-scale commercial venture in the nation. The Federal Reserve System has expanded its credit allocation operations to make itself into an industrial policy fiefdom. And along the way, the U.S. taxpayer has been put on the hook, explicitly or implicitly, for trillions of dollars in new obligations.

POLICY REVOLUTION

Because this book is about our times, these macroeconomic changes have induced us to once again transform this edition of *The Economics of Macro Issues*. For example, the chapters on fiscal policy are broader and deeper than in any prior edition. We also have responded to changes in European economic policy by substantially enlarging the section on globalization and international finance. The result of our revisions, we believe, is a book that addresses more critical new issues with more timeliness and, we hope, more insight than any prior edition. We also believe that we are able to showcase pivotal developments in economic affairs and policymaking in ways that no other book on the market can match.

NEW TO THIS EDITION

The new issues addressed in this edition include the following:

- The Great Stagflation—*why the economic recovery has been so weak*
- Inflation and the Debt Bomb—*why soaring government debt means that inflation* must *go up*
- Who *Really* Pays Taxes?—*contrary to politicians' claims, it's the rich who foot the bill for Uncle Sam*
- Phone It In: The Coming Revolution in the Payments System—*with one swipe of your smart phone, you can soon buy anything*

- Is the Eurozone Zoning Out?—*why not let someone else pay for your troubles?*
- The Global Power of the Big Mac—*how a simple burger illuminates the mysteries of foreign exchange markets*

In addition to completely replacing a substantial portion of the book, all of the remaining chapters have been touched in one way or another by the revision. Moreover, we have continued to improve the questions appearing at the end of each chapter, and done so in a way that will provide both challenge and enlightenment to students at all levels of academic achievement. Quite simply, we have sought to provide a book that reflects in every dimension the major transformations that have taken place in the American economy over the past few years, and to ensure accessibility of the results to all. The result, we believe, will stimulate readers in unprecedented ways.

Instructor's Manual

Every instructor will want to access the *Instructor's Manual* that accompanies *The Economics of Macro Issues*. It is available online to all adopters of the book. For each chapter, the manual provides the following:

- A synopsis that cuts to the core of the economic issues involved in the chapter.
- A concise exposition of the "behind-the-scenes" economic analysis on which the discussion in the text is based. In almost all cases, this exposition is supplemented with one or more diagrams that we have found to be particularly useful as teaching tools.
- Answers to the Discussion Questions posed at the end of the chapter—answers that further develop the basic economic analysis of the chapter and almost always suggest new avenues of discussion.

The Review Team

Of course, an undertaking such as this revision requires an enormous amount of behind-the-scenes activity, and we have been fortunate to have some of the best helpmates imaginable. Reviewers of the last edition contributed considerably to this revision, offering key proposals for new topics and approaches and often e-mailing us with suggestions even as the revision was taking place. They played an integral role in our efforts. Special thanks go to Cyril Morong of San Antonio College for his welcome suggestions.

To all of these individuals, we are grateful. Although we were unable to do everything they wanted, we believe that each of them will be able to see the impact they had on the book. Those professors who participated in this review are Jim Marsis, Salve Regina University; Morris Coats, Nicholls State University; Nancy Short, Duke University; Robert Miller, American River College–Los Rios; John McArthur, Wofford College; Daniel D. Kuester, Kansas State University; Tomi Ovaska, Youngstown State University; Cyril Morong, San Antonio College; David Flint, Texas A&M University; Ronnie Liggett, University of Texas–Arlington.

The Production Team

Our thanks also go to the individuals involved in the hands-on production process. As usual, Sue Jasin of K&M Consulting contributed expert typing and editing, and Robbie Benjamin was unstinting in her demands for clarity of thought and exposition. We also thank our editors at Pearson, Noel Seibert, Carolyn Terbush, and David Alexander, for their encouragement and help in this project.

R.L.M.
D.K.B.

PART ONE

The Miracle of
Economic Growth

CHAPTER **1**

Rich Nation,
Poor Nation

Why do the citizens of some nations grow rich while the inhabitants of others remain poor? Your initial answer might be "because of differences in the **natural-resource endowments** of the nations." It is true that ample endowments of energy, timber, and fertile land all help increase **wealth.** But natural resources can be only a very small part of the answer, as witnessed by many counterexamples. Switzerland and Luxembourg, for example, are nearly devoid of key natural resources, and yet decade after decade, the real income of citizens of those lands has grown rapidly, propelling them to great prosperity. Similarly, Hong Kong, which consists of but a few square miles of rock and hillside, is one of the economic miracles of modern times, while in Russia, a land amply endowed with vast quantities of virtually every important resource, most people remain mired in economic misery.

Unraveling the Mystery of Growth

Recent studies have begun to unravel the mystery of **economic growth.** Repeatedly, they have found that it is the fundamental political and legal **institutions** of society that are conducive to growth. Of these, political stability, secure private property rights, and legal systems based on the **rule of law** are among the most important. Such institutions encourage people to make long-term investments in improvements to land and in all forms of **physical** and **human capital.** These investments raise the **capital stock,** which in turn provides for more growth long into the future. In addition, the cumulative effects of this growth over time eventually yield much higher **standards of living.**

Table 1–1 Differing Legal Systems

Common Law Nations	Civil Law Nations
Australia	Brazil
Canada	Egypt
India	France
Israel	Greece
New Zealand	Italy
United Kingdom	Mexico
United States	Sweden

Professor Paul Mahoney of the University of Virginia, for example, has studied the contrasting effects of different legal systems on economic growth. Many legal systems around the world today are based on one of two models: the English **common law system** and the French **civil law system**. Common law systems reflect a conscious decision in favor of a limited role for government and emphasize the importance of the judiciary in constraining the power of the executive and legislative branches of government. In contrast, civil law systems favor the creation of a strong centralized government in which the legislature and the executive branch have the power to grant preferential treatment to special interests. Table 1–1 shows a sample of common law and civil law nations.

THE IMPORTANCE OF SECURE PROPERTY RIGHTS

Mahoney finds that the security of property rights is much stronger in nations with common law systems, such as the United Kingdom and its former colonies, including the United States. In nations such as France and its former colonies, the civil law systems are much more likely to yield unpredictable changes in the rules of the game—the structure of **property and contract rights.** This, in turn, reduces the willingness of people to make long-term fixed investments in nations with civil law systems, a fact that ultimately slows their growth and lowers the standard of living of their citizens.

The reasoning is simple. If the police will not help you protect your rights to a home or car, you are less likely to acquire those **assets.** Similarly, if you cannot easily enforce business or employment contracts, you are much less likely to enter into those contracts—and thus less likely to produce as many goods or services. Furthermore, if you cannot plan for the future because you do not know what the rules of the game will be ten years or perhaps even one year from now, you are far less likely to make productive long-term investments that require years to pay off. Common law systems seem to do a better job at enforcing contracts and securing property rights and thus would be expected to promote economic activity now and economic growth over time.

When Mahoney examined the economic performance of nations around the world, he found that economic growth has been one-third higher in the common law nations than it has been in civil law nations. Over the three decades covered by his study, the increase in the standard of living—measured by **real per capita income**—was more than 20 percent greater in common law nations than in civil law nations. If such a pattern persisted over the span of a century, it would produce a staggering 80 percent difference in real per capita income in favor of nations with secure property rights.

The Importance of Other Institutions

The economists William Easterly and Ross Levine have taken a much broader view, both across time and across institutions, assessing the economic growth of a variety of nations since their days as colonies. These authors examine how institutions such as political stability, protection of persons and property against violence or theft, security of contracts, and freedom from regulatory burdens contribute to sustained economic growth. They find that it is key institutions such as these, rather than natural-resource endowments, that explain long-term differences in growth and thus present-day differences in levels of real income. To illustrate the powerful effect of institutions, consider the contrast between Mexico, with a real per capita income of about $15,000 today, and the United States, with a real per capita income of about $50,000. Easterly and Levine conclude that if Mexico had developed with the same political and legal institutions that the United States has enjoyed, per capita income in Mexico today would be equal to that in the United States.

The Historical Roots of Today's Institutions

In light of the tremendous importance of institutions in determining long-term growth, Easterly and Levine go on to ask another important question: How have countries gotten the political and legal institutions they have today? The answer has to do with disease, of all things. The seventy-two countries Easterly and Levine examined are all former European colonies in which a variety of colonial strategies were pursued. In Australia, New Zealand, and North America, the colonists found geography and climate that were conducive to good health. Permanent settlement in such locations was attractive, and so the settlers created institutions to protect private property and curb the power of the state. But when Europeans arrived in Africa and South America, they encountered tropical diseases—such as malaria and yellow fever—that produced high mortality among the settlers. This discouraged permanent settlement and encouraged a mentality focused on extracting metals, cash crops, and other resources. This, in turn, provided little incentive to promote democratic institutions or stable long-term property rights systems. The differing initial institutions helped shape economic growth over the years, and their persistence continues to shape the political and legal character and the standard of living in these nations today.

WHY NATIONS FAIL

Scholars Daron Acemoglu and James Robinson have summarized the varieties of institutions found around the world into two broad categories: "inclusive" and "extractive." Nations with inclusive institutions tend to be democracies based on the common law. Most importantly they have legal structures that create incentives for everyone to invest in the future. Nations with extractive institutions are often based on civil law and have centralized government powers, but the key is that their institutions protect the political and economic power of a small elite that takes resources from everyone else.

Acemoglu and Robinson find that whether we look at the sweep of history or the span of nations today, the results are the same. Prosperity is much greater and lasts longer in nations with inclusive institutions compared to those with extractive institutions. Remarkably, the authors conclude that experts cannot engineer prosperity by offering the right advice to rulers on policies or institutions, because rulers actually "get it wrong" on purpose, not by mistake.

Change, and thus prosperity, can happen only when a broad coalition of citizens insist on inclusive institutions. This reasoning leads the authors to a striking conclusion regarding China, where economic growth has been so robust over the last 35 years. Because the Chinese government has maintained tight, centralized political control even while allowing economic freedom in some areas of the country, Acemoglu and Robinson conclude that the economic gains of that nation are unlikely to continue. Indeed, they boldly assert that over the coming decades "the spectacular growth rates in China will slowly evaporate."

NO PROPERTY RIGHTS, NO PROPERTY

Whatever the future of China turns out to be, there is little doubt that extractive political and legal institutions can dramatically alter outcomes in the wrong direction. When Zimbabwe won its independence from Great Britain in 1980, it was one of the most prosperous nations in

Africa. Soon after taking power as Zimbabwe's first (and thus far only) president, Robert Mugabe began disassembling that nation's rule of law, tearing apart the institutions that had helped it grow rich. He reduced the security of property rights in land and eventually confiscated those rights altogether. Mugabe has also gradually taken control of the prices of most goods and services in his nation. The Mugabe government has even confiscated large **stocks** of food and most other things of value that might be exported out of or imported into Zimbabwe. In short, anything that is produced or saved has become subject to confiscation, so the incentives to do either are—to put it mildly—reduced.

As a result, between 1980 and 1996, real per capita income in Zimbabwe fell by one-third, and since 1996 it has fallen by an additional third, and now is only $500. Eighty percent of the workforce is unemployed, investment is nonexistent, and the annual inflation rate reached 231 *million* percent in 2008—just before the monetary system collapsed completely. Decades of labor and capital investment have been destroyed because the very institutions that made progress possible have been eliminated. It is a lesson we ignore at our peril.

FOR CRITICAL ANALYSIS

1. Consider two countries, A and B, and suppose that both have identical *physical* endowments of, say, iron ore. In country A, however, any profits made from mining the ore are subject to confiscation by the government, while in country B, there is no such risk. How does the risk of expropriation affect the *economic* endowments of the two nations? In which nation are people likely to be richer?

2. In light of your answer to question 1, how do you explain the fact that in some countries there is widespread political support for government policies that expropriate resources from some groups for the purpose of handing them out to other groups?

3. Going to college in the United States raises average lifetime earnings by about two-thirds, given our current political and economic institutions. Now suppose that ownership of the added income generated by your college education suddenly became uncertain. Specifically, suppose a law was passed in your state that enabled the governor to select 10 percent of the graduating class from all of the state's colleges and universities each year and impose a tax of up to 50 percent on the difference between the earnings of these people in their first job and the average earnings of people in the state who have only a high school education. What would happen to immigration into

or out of the state? What would happen to attendance at colleges and universities within the state? If the governor were allowed to arbitrarily decide who got hit with the new tax, what would happen to campaign contributions to the governor? What would happen to the number of people "volunteering" to work in the governor's next campaign? Would your decision to invest in a college education change? Explain your responses.

4. Go to a source such as the CIA *World Factbook* or the World Bank and collect per capita income and population data for each of the nations listed in Table 1–1. Compare the average per capita income of the common law nations with the average per capita income of the civil law countries. Based on the discussion in this chapter, identify at least two other factors that you think are important to take into account when assessing whether the differences you observe are likely due to the systems of the countries.

5. Most international attempts to aid people living in low-income nations have come in one of two forms: (i) gifts of consumer goods (such as food), and (ii) assistance in constructing or obtaining capital goods (such as tractors or dams or roads). Based on what you have learned in this chapter, how likely are such efforts to *permanently* raise the standard of living in such countries? Explain.

6. Louisiana and Quebec both have systems of local law (state and provincial, respectively) that are heavily influenced by their common French heritage, which includes civil law. What do you predict is true about per capita income in Louisiana compared to the other U.S. states, and per capita income in Quebec, compared to the other Canadian provinces? Is this prediction confirmed by the facts (which can be readily ascertained with a few quick Web searches)? Identify at least two other factors that you think are important to take into account when assessing whether the differences you observe are likely due to the influence of civil law institutions.

CHAPTER **2**

Outsourcing and Economic Growth

One prominent business commentator keeps a "hit list" of corporations that send jobs overseas. Such actions are decidedly un-American, he opines, whenever he gets a chance to express his views against **outsourcing.** A recent Democratic presidential nominee had a name for heads of companies that outsourced telemarketing projects, customer services, and other white-collar jobs to foreign countries: He called them "Benedict Arnold CEOs."

Congress even tried to pass a bill to prevent any type of outsourcing by the Department of State and the Department of Defense. Republican representative Don Manzullo of Illinois said, "You can't just continue to outsource overseas time after time after time, lose your strategic military base, and then expect this Congress to sit back and see the jobs lost and do nothing." When an adviser to the president publicly stated that the foreign outsourcing of service jobs was not such a bad idea, numerous politicians lambasted him for even the suggestion that outsourcing could be viewed in a positive light.

What Is This "Outsourcing?"

The concept of outsourcing is simple: Instead of hiring American workers at home, American corporations hire foreign workers to do the same jobs. For example, some of these foreign workers are in India and do call center work, answering technical questions for computer purchasers. Another job such workers do well (and cheaply) is software development and debugging. Because of low-cost communication, especially over the Internet, software programmers can be just about anywhere in the world and still work for U.S. corporations.

Besides the fear that outsourcing "robs Americans of jobs," it is also claimed that outsourcing reduces **economic growth** in the United States. (Presumably, that must mean that it increases economic growth in, say, India.) Because outsourcing is part and parcel of international trade in goods and services, the real question becomes: Can the United States have higher growth rates if it restricts American corporations from "sending jobs abroad?"

As we set out to answer this question, we must keep one simple fact in mind: Outsourcing is nothing more or less than the purchase of labor services from the residents of a foreign nation. When the Detroit Red Wings host the Vancouver Canucks, fans at the game are outsourcing: They are purchasing labor services from Canadians. In this sense, Canadian hockey players are no different from Indian software engineers. They are citizens of foreign nations who are competing with citizens of the United States in the supply of labor services. Just as important, outsourcing is no different from any other form of international trade.

THE LINK BETWEEN ECONOMIC GROWTH AND OUTSOURCING

International trade has been around for thousands of years. That means that the concept of outsourcing is certainly not new, even though the term seems to be. After all, the exchange of services between countries is a part of international trade. In any event, if we decide to restrict this type of international trade in services, we will be restricting international trade in general. Experts who study economic growth today have found that the openness of an economy is a key determinant of its rate of economic growth. Any restriction on outsourcing is a type of **trade barrier,** one that will reduce the benefits we obtain from international trade.

There is a clear historical link between economic growth and trade barriers. Figure 2–1 shows the relationship between the openness of an economy—fewer or more trade barriers—and the rate of economic growth. Along the horizontal axis of the graph is a trade barrier index, which for the United States is equal to 100. On the vertical axis, you see the average annual growth of **per capita income** in percentage terms.

It is evident from this graph that countries that have fewer international trade barriers have also had higher rates of economic growth. The lesson of history is quite clear: International trade increases economic growth, and growth boosts economic well-being. Government efforts to restrict outsourcing will restrict international trade, and this will make Americans poorer, not richer.

Figure 2–1 Relationship between Economic Growth and Barriers to
International Trade

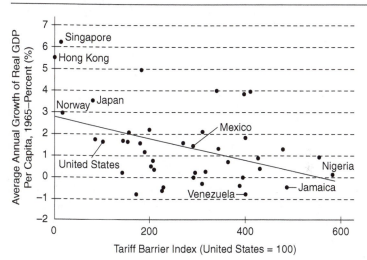

Tariff Barrier Index (United States = 100)

WILL THE UNITED STATES BECOME A
THIRD WORLD COUNTRY?

In spite of the evidence just shown, Paul Craig Roberts, a former Reagan administration treasury official, declared at a Brookings Institution conference that "the United States will be a Third World country in twenty years." His prediction was based on the idea that entire classes of high-wage service-sector employees will eventually find themselves in competition with highly skilled workers abroad who earn much less than their U.S. counterparts. He contended that U.S. software programmers and radiologists, for example, will not be able to compete in the global economy. Thus, he argued, the United States will lose millions of white-collar jobs due to outsourcing of service-sector employment to India and China.

Jeffrey E. Garten, former dean of the Yale School of Management, reiterated and expanded on this prediction. He believes that the transfer of jobs abroad will accelerate for generations to come. He argues that in countries from China to the Czech Republic, there is a "virtually unlimited supply of industrious and educated labor working at a fraction of U.S. wages." Similarly, according to Craig Barrett, former board chair at the chipmaker Intel, American workers today face the prospect of "300 million well-educated people in India, China, and Russia who can do effectively any job that can be done" in the United States.

Still other commentators have claimed that India alone will soak up as many as 4 million jobs from the U.S. labor market within the next few years. Some even believe that this number may exceed 10 million. If true, one might expect American software developers and call center technicians to start moving to India!

SOME OVERLOOKED FACTS

Much of the outsourcing discussion has ignored two simple facts that turn out to be important if we really want to understand what the future will bring.

1. *Outsourcing is the result of trade liberalization in foreign nations.* After decades of isolation, the markets in China, India, and Eastern Europe have begun to open up to international trade. As often happens when governments finally allow their people to trade internationally, these governments have pushed hard to stimulate exports—of labor services as well as goods. Nonetheless, this cannot be a long-term equilibrium strategy because the workers producing those goods and supplying those services are doing it because they want to become consumers. Soon enough, and this is already happening, they want to spend their hard-earned income on goods and services, many of which are produced abroad. Thus, today's outsourcing of jobs to those nations is turning into exports of goods and services to those same nations.

2. *Prices adjust to keep markets in balance.* The supply curve of labor is upward-sloping. Thus, as U.S. corporations hire foreign workers (either directly by outsourcing or indirectly by importing goods), market wages in foreign lands must rise. Between 2003 and 2010, for example, Indian labor-outsourcing companies saw wages rise more than 50 percent. Over a longer span, real wages in southern China (which has been open to trade far longer than India) are now *six times higher* than they were just twenty years ago. These higher wages obviously reduce the competitiveness of the firms that must pay them. Moreover, it is not just wages that adjust: The relative values of national currencies move, too. Between 2003 and 2007, the value of the dollar fell more than 25 percent, making foreign goods (and workers) more expensive here and making U.S. goods and workers more attractive in foreign markets.

Of course, adjustments are never instantaneous. Moreover, they are occurring because some American firms are moving output and employment abroad. Hence, at least some U.S. workers are having to move to lower-paying jobs, often with a spell of unemployment along the way. How big is the impact in the short run, before all of the price adjustments take place? According to the Bureau of Labor Statistics, in a typical recent year, the number of jobs lost to outsourcing is measured in the thousands—out of a workforce of over 155 million. So if you are currently a U.S. software developer, you do not have to worry about packing your bags for Mumbai, at least not soon.

INSOURCING BY FOREIGN FIRMS

U.S. firms are not the only ones that engage in outsourcing. Many foreign firms do the same. When a foreign firm outsources to the United States, we can call it **insourcing.** For example, Mexican firms routinely send data to U.S. accounting businesses for calculation of payrolls and for maintaining financial records. Many foreign hospitals pay American radiologists to read X-rays and MRI images. Foreign firms use American firms to provide a host of other services, many of which involve consulting. Also, when a foreign automobile manufacturer builds an assembly plant in the United States, it is in effect outsourcing automobile assembly to American workers. Thus, American workers in the South Carolina BMW plant, the Alabama Mercedes-Benz plant, or the Toyota or Honda plants in Tennessee and Ohio are all beneficiaries of the fact that those foreign companies have outsourced jobs to the United States.

Indeed, all across the country and around the world, hundreds of millions of workers are employed by "foreign" corporations—although it is becoming difficult to tell the nationality of any company, given the far-flung nature of today's global enterprises.

WHAT REALLY MATTERS: THE LONG RUN

If you own the only grocery store in your small town, you are clearly harmed if a competing store opens across the street. If you work in a small telephone equipment store and a large company starts taking away business via Internet sales, you will obviously be worse off. If you formerly were employed at a call center for customer service at Walmart and have just lost your job because Walmart outsourced to a cheaper Indian firm, you will have to look for a new job.

These kinds of "losses" of income or jobs have occurred since the beginning of commerce. They will always exist in any dynamic economy. Indeed, if we look over the American economy as a whole, in a typical year roughly *1 million workers lose their jobs every week.* But in a typical year slightly *more* than 1 million people find a new job every week. On balance then, employment in the United States keeps growing, even though the average person will change jobs every three years—some, no doubt, because of international competition. Job turnover like this is an essential component of a labor market that is continually adjusting to economic change. It is a sign of health, not sickness, in the economy. If you find this hard to believe, you can look west or east. In Japan, efforts to "protect" workers from international trade resulted in economic stagnation and have depressed real income growth over the past twenty years. In Europe, similar efforts to "preserve" the jobs of existing workers have resulted in *higher*, not lower, unemployment because firms are unwilling to hire people that they cannot later fire.

It is true that the pattern of job losses and gains in a given year is altered during an economic recession, such as the latest one. In particular, during the early stages of a recession, additional people lose their jobs in a given week and fewer people find a job each week, with the result being higher unemployment in the short run. But international trade is not the cause of recessions in the United States (although an economic recession can be made worse by *restrictions* on international trade, as it was in the early 1930s). On the contrary, international trade is an important source of economic prosperity.

If you are still wondering, simply look back at Figure 2–1. The lessons of history and of economics are clear: Trade creates **wealth,** and that is true whether the trade is interpersonal, interstate, or international. The reality is that labor outsourcing is simply part of a worldwide trend toward increased international trade in both goods and services. As international trade expands—assuming that politicians and bureaucrats allow it to expand—the result will be higher rates of growth and higher levels of income in the United States and elsewhere. American workers will continue to enjoy the fruits of that growth, just as they always have.

FOR CRITICAL ANALYSIS

1. What, if any, differences exist between competition among service workers across the fifty states and competition among service workers across nations?

2. When BMW decides to build a plant in the United States, who gains and who loses?

3. International Business Machines Corporation (IBM) recently stated that it expected to save almost $170 million annually by shifting several thousand high-paying programming jobs overseas. Explain

why IBM would undertake this move. Then explain the short-run and long-run effects of this outsourcing.

4. Some companies that outsourced call centers during the 1990s have returned these centers to North America over the past decade. Who has gained and who has lost as a result of the return of the call centers to this continent? Explain.

5. The automaker BMW, whose corporate headquarters is in Germany, makes its X-series sport utility vehicles in South Carolina, and sells many of them in China. Who is outsourcing what to whom? Explain.

6. What is the difference between outsourcing and international trade?

CHAPTER 3

Poverty, Capitalism, and Growth

Fifty years ago, nearly half of the world's population lived in abject poverty; today, the proportion is about 17 percent. In fact, compared to fifty years ago, even though the world's population has doubled, there are actually far fewer people now living below the poverty line. Despite the human misery that is evident to varying degrees in virtually every nation of the world, there is little doubt that economic prosperity has made great strides.

THE SWEEP OF HISTORY

The past half-century is but a small part of a story that has evolved over the course of 250 years or so. In the middle of the eighteenth century, perhaps 90 percent of the world's population lived in a state of **abject poverty,** subsisting on the equivalent of less than $450 per person per year, measured in today's terms. In fact, for most of human history, abject poverty—including inadequate nutrition and rudimentary shelter—was the norm for almost everyone, everywhere. This began to change in the eighteenth century with the **Industrial Revolution** and its associated mechanization of tasks that had always been laboriously done by humans or animals. Stimulated in the early years by the invention and application of the steam engine, the Industrial Revolution initiated a massive cascade of innovations in transportation, chemistry, biology, manufacturing processes, communications, and electronic technology. This continuing process of invention and innovation has made little headway in many parts of the world, but where it has taken hold, there has been a sustained rise in average **real per capita income** and a corresponding decline in poverty. By 1820, the extent of abject poverty had fallen from 90 to 80 percent. By 1900, it had dipped below 70 percent and has continued to decline since. Before the Industrial Revolution, more than five out of six people lived in abject poverty. Today, it is one out of six.

UNEVEN PROGRESS

This story of human progress has been uneven across countries. Europe, North America, and a few other locations have witnessed the greatest increases in real per capita income and the greatest decreases in poverty. By contrast, the **standard of living** and the extent of poverty in many African nations have changed little over the past 250 years. Even within given countries, progress has sometimes been erratic. Ninety years ago, for example, the standard of living in Argentina was the sixth highest in the world. Today, that nation ranks 70th in living standards. In contrast, thirty years ago, 750 million people in China lived in abject poverty; that number has since been cut to about 180 million.

In Chapter 1, you saw the key institutional factors that determine average levels of **per capita income.** Secure **property and contract rights** and the **rule of law** were the **institutions** under which the Industrial Revolution flourished best, and it is thus in nations that have embraced these institutions that people are most likely to be prosperous. These same institutions are the ones typically associated with **capitalism,** economic systems that depend primarily (though not necessarily completely) on markets to allocate scarce **resources.** Of course, no country in the world is completely capitalist. In the United States, for example, only about 60 percent of resources are allocated by the private sector, while the rest are allocated by federal, state, or local governments. At the other end of the spectrum, even in Communist countries such as Cuba, Vietnam, and North Korea, markets play at least some role in allocating resources.

Despite a few ambiguities, then, it is possible to measure the degree of capitalism (or, as some would term it, economic freedom) in each country around the world. Doing so yields measures that seem to correspond reasonably well with what many people would think is true about the economies of those countries. For example, using the measures constructed by Canada's Fraser Institute, Hong Kong's economy is rated the most capitalist. Singapore, Switzerland, New Zealand, Canada, and Australia are other nations whose economies are judged among the ten most capitalist in the world. If you know much about economic prosperity around the world, you will be aware that these countries are also among the world leaders in real per capita income. Indeed, the association of capitalism with prosperity is everywhere quite strong.

You may be surprised that the United States was not mentioned among the top ten capitalist nations. In fact, it used to be there, year after year. Beginning about 2005, however, the combination of rapidly growing government regulations and sharply higher federal spending began taking their toll on economic freedom. As a result the United States has dropped from sixth most capitalist to eighteenth on the list. The United States is still slightly more capitalist than Norway or Sweden, but it has fallen behind Denmark and Finland, among many others.

CAPITALISM AND PROSPERITY

When thinking about the impact of capitalism, it is convenient to divide all the nations in the world into four groups, ranging from "most capitalist" to "least capitalist." Data limitations prevent doing this with every single nation. Nevertheless, it is possible to do it for about 140 of them, putting 35 nations into each of the four groups. Thus, among the top thirty-five "most capitalist" nations, in addition to the countries we mentioned earlier, many (but not all!) of the original members of the **European Union (EU)** would be included, along with Chile, Kuwait, and Japan. At the other end of the spectrum, the economies of Iran, Ukraine, Venezuela, and Zimbabwe would all fall into the group of the thirty-five "least capitalist" nations.

As we suggested earlier, people who live in the most capitalist nations in the world also tend to have the highest average income. For example, average per capita income for people living in the group including the thirty-five most capitalist nations averages over $31,000 per year. For people living in the next most capitalist group of nations, per capita income averages about $14,000 per year. Once we get down to the thirty-five least capitalist nations, average income has dropped to but $3,900 per year. In addition, because rates of economic growth are *also* higher in more capitalist nations, the differences in income between the most and least capitalist nations are growing over time.[1]

Of course, this is a chapter about poverty, and the *average* income in a nation may bear little relation to the income earned by its poorest residents. Many people believe, for example, that capitalist nations promote excessively competitive behavior so that people who are not good at competing end up much poorer in capitalist than in noncapitalist nations. If the rich get richer in capitalist countries while the poor get poorer, then

---

1 All income comparisons are made using a method called **purchasing power parity (PPP)**, generally acknowledged to be the most accurate means of making comparisons across nations with very different income levels and consumption bundles.

even if the average person in capitalist nations is doing well, the same might not be true for people at the bottom of the income distribution. As it turns out, however, the poor do *not* do worse in capitalist countries. In fact, they do *better.*

CAPITALISM AND POVERTY

Consider the thirty-five most capitalist nations in the world. On average, the poorest 10 percent of the population receives about 2.5 percent of total income in these countries. Indeed, if we look across *all* countries, we find that although there is some variation from nation to nation, the poorest 10 percent of the population typically gets between 2.0 and 2.5 percent of total income. One way to put this is that on average, capitalism does *not* lower the share of total income going to the people at the bottom of the income distribution. Capitalist or Communist, in Africa or in the Americas, the per capita income of the poorest 10 percent of the population in a nation ends up being about one-quarter of per capita income in the middle of the income distribution for that country.

Now if you followed the numbers earlier about average income and capitalism, you may already have figured out the next point: Because capitalism raises total income in a nation without reducing the *share* of income going to the poor, capitalism ends up raising income at *all* points in the income distribution. Thus, for the poorest 10 percent of the population in highly capitalist countries, average per capita income is about $8,700 per year (or just under $35,000 per year for a family of four). For the poorest 10 percent of the population in the least capitalist countries, average income is under $950 per year (about $3,800 for a family of four). Expressed somewhat differently, poor people in the most capitalist nations can expect average income levels *eight times higher* than poor people in the least capitalist nations.

NOW AND THE FUTURE

The radically better standard of living experienced by the poor in capitalist nations is reflected in many other statistics indicative of quality of life. For example, life expectancy in the thirty-five most capitalist nations is about 79 years. In the least capitalist, it is about 58. Similarly, infant mortality rates are *eight times higher* in the least capitalist countries than in the most capitalist countries. Moreover, because people at the top of the income distribution have access to health care in both rich and poor nations, these differences in life expectancy and infant mortality are chiefly due to differences among people at the bottom of the income distribution. In capitalist nations, compared to noncapitalist countries, it is the poor whose newborns are surviving infancy and whose adults are surviving to old age.

There is another compelling difference between capitalist and noncapitalist countries that sheds light on what the future may bring. In the thirty-five most capitalist countries of the world, fewer than 1 percent of children under the age of 15 are working rather than in school. In the thirty-five least capitalist nations, one child of every six under the age of 15 is working rather than being in school—a rate nearly twenty times higher. Thus, in capitalist nations, children are much more likely to be getting the education needed to acquire the skills of the future. This in turn means that **economic growth** is likely to be higher in capitalist nations than in noncapitalist nations, and this is exactly what we observe. Growth in per capita income in the thirty-five most capitalist countries averages about 2.3 percent per year, enough to double income at all levels over the next 30 years. In contrast, average per capita incomes are actually *falling* in the least capitalist countries, implying that the misery of today's poor in these nations is likely to get worse.

MORE THAN NUMBERS

It is easy to get too wrapped up in numbers, so it may be useful to make a few simple head-to-head comparisons. Consider North Korea and South Korea. Both emerged from World War II with shattered economies, only to fight each other in the Korean War. When the war was over, South Korea embraced capitalism, building an economy based on the rule of law, secure property rights, and a reliance on the market as the primary means of allocating scarce resources. North Korea rejected all of these, choosing instead a Communist system that relied on centralized command and control to allocate resources—a system ruled not by law but by one man at the top. South Korea became a world economic powerhouse, with per capita income of almost $32,000 per year. North Korea stagnated and, with a per capita income of only $1,800 per year, must now rely on foreign aid to feed many of its people.

If we were to look at East Germany and West Germany between World War II and the fall of the Berlin Wall in 1989, we would see the same story repeated. West Germany embraced the central principles of a market-based capitalist economy and prospered. East Germany rejected those principles, and its people were impoverished. A similar tale of two countries can be told in comparing the economies of Taiwan and China between 1950 and 1980. Capitalist Taiwan prospered while Communist China stagnated—and people at the bottom of the income distribution suffered the most.

Indeed, China itself presents us with a tale of two countries, the Communist version before 1980 and the increasingly capitalist one of the years since. After decades of post–World War II stagnation under communism, the gradual move toward market-based resource allocation in China since 1980 is transforming life for people at all levels of income. Overall, real per capita income has roughly doubled every decade since 1980. Moreover, at least in those areas of the country where the Communists have let the capitalists try their hand, this economic progress has been widespread and sustained. Thus, even though political freedom in China is not yet to be had, the growing economic freedom in that nation is having the same impact it has had around the world and over time: When people are able to enjoy secure property rights, the rule of law, and a reliance on markets as allocators of scarce resources, people at *all* points in the distribution benefit.

FOR CRITICAL ANALYSIS

1. The income measures discussed in this chapter do not include non-cash benefits that are often available to low-income individuals, such as food stamps and Medicaid. Do you think such noncash benefits are more likely to be made available to poor people in a rich nation or in a poor nation? Explain your answer. (*Hint:* Do people get more or less charitable as their incomes rise?) Then ask yourself, how will the difference in noncash benefits in rich nations versus poor nations affect your conclusions regarding relative incomes of poor individuals in capitalist nations compared to noncapitalist nations? Explain this answer as well.

2. How would a political system in which there is the rule of law (i.e., in which the same rules apply to everyone) serve to protect people at the bottom of the income distribution most strongly?

3. In light of the analysis in Chapter 1 and the information presented in this chapter, what are some ways that people in developed nations might help people in developing nations achieve higher income levels? Give specific examples.

4. If capitalism is so good at creating economic prosperity, why don't more nations try it?

5. Over the past few years, the United States has slipped downward in the rankings of capitalist countries. As you read the rest of this book, use the knowledge you gain to compile a list of the specific reasons you think the U.S. ranking has dropped.

6. According to the CIA *World Factbook*, the Democratic Republic of the Congo is the poorest nation in the world, with per capita income at $300 per year. How do you suppose this country ranks in its degree of capitalism? Test your prediction by going to the Fraser Institute's Web site (www.fraserinstitute.org) and seeing where the Congo rates on the Institute's Index of Economic Freedom.

CHAPTER 4

The Threat to Growth

Government spending has hit levels virtually unprecedented in American history. The federal government, for example, has been spending fully *one-quarter* of gross domestic product (GDP), and state and local governments have been spending nearly as much. Local government spending, for example, has accounted for 10 percent of GDP, while state governments have been spending about 12.5 percent. At no time in American history have state and local governments spent as much as they have been recently. Only briefly, during the height of World War II, has federal spending as a share of GDP ever rivaled its recent heights. Bailouts, subsidies, entitlements, bloated pensions, subsidized health care, and two ground wars in Asia (Iraq and Afghanistan) have created a "perfect storm" of massive government spending at all levels.

THE BIG PICTURE

"So what," you might say. If the government was not spending it, someone else would be. Indeed, when government spends more, whatever the spending is on, there is ultimately only one place the government can obtain the resources. That place is you and everyone else who earns income each year in the United States. In the short run, just as you can borrow, so too can governments, an activity that is called running a **budget deficit.** Nevertheless, the ability to borrow does not change the fundamental **budget constraint** facing our society. What is spent today must be paid for now or in the future. And when it is government doing the spending, that means the higher spending today *must* eventually be matched with higher taxes. Hence, today's big spending means higher taxes (and lower private spending) for you and everyone else who earns income in the United States.

Now, if those higher taxes just meant that Peter would have less spending power so that Paul could have more, this chapter probably would not be worth writing. But Peter's income does not simply appear like a surprise birthday gift. Instead, his income is the result of hard work, investing, and innovation. When taxes rise, the **incentives** of taxpayers to work, invest, and innovate is reduced—and that in turn means lower economic growth and lower wealth now and in the future.

INCENTIVES ARE IMPORTANT

We have seen in the previous chapters that secure property rights and the rule of law are crucial in fostering economic growth. These institutions help ensure that individuals are secure in the knowledge that they will get to keep the fruits of their labor. Hence, people are willing to work hard, invest for the future, and engage in innovation. In addition, because all of these activities contribute to higher incomes and greater economic growth, they ensure more long-run prosperity. But note the key point: People work, invest, and innovate because they believe they will be rewarded with the fruits of their efforts. If these fruits are denied them—because, for example, taxes take much of what they produce— the incentives to work, invest, and innovate are sharply reduced, and so too is economic growth and, ultimately, wealth.

Data from Europe illustrate how taxes shape incentives to work. Researchers have found that a tax increase of just over 12 percentage points induces the average adult in Europe to reduce work effort by over 120 hours per year—the equivalent of almost four weeks' work. Such a tax change also causes a sharp reduction in the number of people who work at all, and causes many others to join the **underground economy** or to devote their time to **tax evasion.** Overall, then, higher tax rates cause lower output and higher unemployment. Wealth is reduced now and in the future.

Taxes also affect the incentives to invest. A good case in point is Ireland, whose economy in the 1980s was a disaster and whose citizens were among the poorest of **European Union (EU)** citizens. In the 1990s, the Irish slashed the corporate **profits** tax to 12.5 percent, the lowest in Europe and only about one-third as high as the U.S. rate of 35 percent. Beginning in 2004, the Irish government also began offering a 20 percent tax credit for company spending on research and development, offering high-tech firms an opportunity to cut their taxes by starting up and expanding operations in Ireland. Almost immediately, Ireland became a magnet for new investment and for successful companies that did not want to hand over one-third or more of their profits to the tax collector.

The combination of lower corporate tax rates and tax breaks on research and development induced hundreds of multinational corporations to begin operations in Ireland. They brought with them hundreds of thousands of new jobs (and this to a nation of only 4 million residents), and Ireland quickly became number one among the **EU's** fifteen original members in being home to companies that conduct research and development. As for the people of Ireland, their per capita incomes went from the bottom ranks of the EU to the top.[1]

INNOVATION IS ESSENTIAL

On one point, all economists agree: Innovation is a fundamental, indeed necessary, element of economic growth. Note that we say "innovation" rather than "invention." The latter is the creation of a new idea—but plenty of new ideas go nowhere. Innovation is the transformation of a new idea into successful commercial, scientific, or artistic application. Although innovation may incorporate invention, it need not do so. A simple example may suffice.

Many people credit Thomas Edison with the invention in 1880 of the incandescent light bulb. In fact, the first recognizable incandescent bulb was created in 1802 by Sir Humphry Davy and a bulb very much like Edison's was patented in 1875 by two Canadians. Shortly after Edison independently patented an incandescent bulb, he bought the Canadians' patent rights from them for $5,000 (over $1 million in today's dollars)—and then proceeded to implement indoor electric lighting across America and around the world. The invention was the incandescent light bulb. The innovation entailed the successful commercial application of that invention, an activity that included power generation and transmission, as well as the widespread commercial distribution of the bulbs themselves. Sitting in an English, Canadian, or New Jersey laboratory, the bulb was a bright idea. Once it lit up millions of homes and workplaces, however, it raised the world's wealth and contributed to sustained economic growth that continues to enrich us today.

INNOVATION AND WEALTH

Steve Jobs (Apple) did not invent the semiconductor, Bill Gates (Microsoft) did not invent the computer operating system, Oprah Winfrey (The Oprah Show) did not invent the talk show, and Mark Zuckerberg (Facebook) did not invent social networking. Yet each of

---

1 Sadly for the Irish, their government decided to spend much of this higher income bailing out mismanaged Irish banks who overinvested in commercial and residential real estate before the recession of 2007–2009.

these people became multi-billionaires as innovators in their respective fields of work. To be sure, each has come up with plenty of new ideas, but what distinguishes them from all of the inventors you have never heard of is that the people on the list above have developed and applied their ideas and others' in ways that created enormous commercial success. In doing so, each got rich. More importantly for our purposes, they have contributed significantly to the wealth of millions of *other* people around the world, by creating products that satisfied human wants.

Indeed, if we look more carefully at the world, we find that innovation is the source of most of our wealth. It could be the Mexican farmers who 6,000 years ago began genetically engineering the precursors to corn. Or it might be Bill Hewlett and David Packard, who transformed semiconductors into calculators, business machines, and laser printers. But in each instance, it is innovation that has created the products that enable us to live like no other species on earth. In addition, although it is unlikely that many of the long-dead creators of corn got rich, many of the richest people in the world are rich because of their innovations.

Even among the merely prosperous people of the world, innovation often plays a key role in creating their prosperity. Although **wealth** is obviously passed down from one generation to another, when we look at the **standard of living** of individuals, very little of that standard of living is determined by the financial inheritance they received from their ancestors. Instead, current living standards of people are primarily determined by the incomes they have earned for themselves. These incomes are chiefly the result of what they have produced in the workplace.[2] And most often, very high levels of workplace productivity are the result of innovative activity by those productive individuals.

TAXATION AND INNOVATION

Surely many things motivate all individuals, including innovators, great and small. One of these motivating factors may reasonably be assumed to be financial success. (We say this because there is a vast body of evidence that financial success is one of the motivators of human beings in virtually all walks of life.) This notion brings us back to taxes, where our story began. Innovators, like everyone else, only receive **after-tax income,** that

---

2 We do inherit plenty of nonfinancial wealth from our parents, of course, including intelligence and work habits, which play a role in determining how much we produce and hence our standard of living. The impact of productivity on prosperity is most obvious when we look at professional sports, where pay is quite obviously determined by easily measurable criteria of productivity (such as touchdowns, home runs, or rebounds).

is, income *after* the various government entities have collected the taxes they impose. These taxes may come in a variety of forms: income taxes, sales taxes, property taxes, and so forth. Whatever their form or level of government at which they are levied, however, higher taxes mean lower after-tax incomes, and this reduces the incentive to innovate. Higher taxes also reduce the incentive to invest (because taxes cut into the after-tax income from investment) and even to work—because higher taxes mean lower after-tax income from work. Across the board, then, higher taxes discourage the very activities that create prosperity.

An easy way to think about the effect of taxes on behavior is to imagine that we decided to raise taxes on professional athletes. Recall from above that the most productive people are those who tend to earn the highest incomes. Almost surely, then, the biggest burden of higher taxes would be on those with the highest incomes—which also means those who are the most productive. The best runners and rebounders and hitters and passers would get the biggest increase in tax bills. What are the likely consequences? Overall performance would suffer. Athletes would spend less time working out in the off-season. They would spend less time practicing year round. They would devote less effort to studying their opponents—the list goes on and on. And the result would be a decline in the quality of the competition and less enjoyment for fans. Output, no matter how we measure it, would fall. To be sure, many players would still be motivated by pride and inherent competitive drive, but the extra edge offered by financial rewards would be gone—and so would the performance edge.

The same destruction of incentives occurs when taxes are raised on anyone who works, or invests, or innovates. As long as incomes are determined chiefly by performance (and the evidence is that they are), higher taxes reduce the incentive of people to engage in those activities that contribute to economic growth and thus increase our wealth. As in sports, the outcome is reduced performance and lower output, however measured.

THE RELEVANCE FOR TODAY

We started this chapter by discussing the historically high levels of government spending that we have been experiencing. Because this spending must eventually be paid for out of taxes, we can now see the threat to economic growth and prosperity that is posed by high levels of government spending. The result of this spending *must* be higher taxes, and higher taxes will reduce the incentives to work, invest, and innovate. This in turn means less economic growth and lower income and wealth. Our standard of living in the future will be lowered because of our governments' spending today.

Nearly a half century ago, President John F. Kennedy said, "An economy hampered by restrictive taxes will never produce enough revenue to balance our budget, just as it will never produce enough jobs or enough profits." Sadly, this is a message that our current political leaders do not seem to understand.

FOR CRITICAL ANALYSIS

1. Barack Obama campaigned for the presidency on the theme that he would bring "change" to the United States. One of the major changes occurring in President Obama's first term in office was in the size of the federal debt. Largely because of higher federal spending over those years, federal debt rose 60 percent (an increase of about $19,000 for each person living in the United States). What does this higher debt imply must happen to the taxes you will pay over your lifetime?

2. Many European countries have imposed a **wealth tax.** It is typically based on everything a person owns, minus everything the person owes (the difference between what is owned and what is owed is called **net worth**). Put yourself in the shoes of an individual in a country that has just decided to impose a wealth tax. How does a wealth tax affect your incentive to accumulate wealth? How does it affect your incentive to work hard?

3. Explain why the incentives of individuals and businesses are chiefly affected by changes in **marginal tax rates**—that is, the share of the *next* income earned that must go to taxes.

4. Fifty years ago in the United States, high-income people paid 91 cents in federal personal income taxes on each additional dollar of income they earned. If you found yourself paying such a 91 marginal tax rate, how great would be your incentive to find legal **loopholes** to reduce your federal tax **liabilities?** If you found yourself in the lowest federal personal income tax bracket of, say, 15 percent (paying 15 cents in taxes out of each additional dollar earned), would your incentive to find loopholes to reduce your tax bill be the same? Explain.

5. Let's suppose that income tax rates rise significantly over the next ten years. How can people at all levels of income react over time, not just immediately after taxes are raised? How will the size of the

response differ, say, a year after the rise in tax rates compared to a week after the increase? Is it possible that some people will actually change their behavior *before* the higher tax rates go into effect? Explain.

6. How does the structure of a country's tax system affect who decides to immigrate into the nation or emigrate out of the nation? Contrast, for example, nations A and B. Assume that nation A applies a 20 percent tax rate on every dollar of income earned by an individual (i.e., 20 cents in taxes must be paid on each dollar of income). Nation B applies a 10 percent tax rate (10 cents per dollar) on the *first* $40,000 per year of income and a 40 percent tax rate (40 cents per dollar) on all income *above* $40,000 per year earned by an individual. Start by computing the tax bill in each country that must be paid by a person earning $40,000 per year and the tax bill that must be paid by a person earning $100,000 per year. Then consider the more general issue: If the language, culture, and climate of the two nations are similar, and if a person can choose to live on one side or the other of a river separating the two nations, who is more likely to choose to live in A, and who is more likely to choose to live in B? To what extent does your reasoning apply if an ocean, rather than a river, separates the two countries? Does it apply if the language, culture, or climate in the two nations differs? Explain.

PART TWO

The Business Cycle, Unemployment, and Inflation

CHAPTER **5**

Is GDP What
We Want?

Economists disagree about a lot. One important point of disagreement has to do with how to measure things. For example, suppose you were interested in how the economy was doing, either over time or in comparison to other nations. Or perhaps you want to know how well different people across the country feel they are doing. The most common way of addressing such issues would be with a measure linked to **gross domestic product (GDP).** For example, almost all macroeconomic policy is driven by policymakers' perceptions of what is happening to a few key variables, and GDP is on just about everyone's list of key variables. Moreover, as you saw in Chapter 3, the human condition varies dramatically around the globe. Radical differences in prosperity and poverty from one nation to the next can be understood only if we begin with a clear awareness of what is being measured. That measurement starts with GDP.

What Does GDP Measure?

GDP is defined as the market value of new, domestically produced, final goods and services. There are four key elements of this definition:

1. *Market value*—GDP is calculated by multiplying the prices of goods and services by their quantities. Thus, it can rise or fall just because of changes in the prices of goods and service. Most of our discussion will focus on **real GDP,** which adjusts GDP for changes in the **price level.** This way, we know that we are talking about the actual amounts of goods and services that are being produced.

2. *New*—The only goods and services that get into GDP are ones that are newly produced during the current accounting period, which

normally is the current calendar year. Even though used cars, old houses, and even antiques are a source of satisfaction for many people, GDP focuses on those goods and services that are currently produced.

3. *Domestically produced*—If you were to look carefully at the components of a new car, you would find that much of that car was actually made in other nations, even if it is an "American" car. Similarly, much of the typical "Japanese" car sold in America is actually made in America. The GDP of a nation includes only those parts of cars (and other goods and services) that are made in that nation.

4. *Final goods and services*—Lots of intermediate steps go into producing goods and services, and typically many of these steps show up as separate transactions across the country. Nonetheless, because the value of each intermediate step is embedded in the value of the final product, we include only that final value in our measure of GDP. Otherwise, we would be double-counting the final good and all of the components that go into it.

IMPUTED AND MISSING INFORMATION

Real GDP, that is, GDP corrected for changes in the price level, is the official measure of the new, domestically produced, final goods and services in an economy. Although this number is widely used for many purposes, you should be aware of its limitations. First, some important parts of it are "imputed," or estimated, by the officials at the government agency that publishes the GDP numbers. For example, even though there is no "market" in owner-occupied housing, the Commerce Department has devised methods of estimating the implicit rental value of houses occupied by their owners, and it includes the aggregate value of these services in the published measure of real GDP. In a similar vein, farmers consume some of the food items they produce before those items ever get to the market. Again, the Commerce Department has devised ways to estimate the amount of such food. As with owner-occupied housing, these estimates are included in the official GDP numbers.

Despite the government's best efforts, there are some major omissions from published measures of real GDP. For example, do-it-yourself activities are not included in the official measures, even though they constitute the production of a service. If you take your car to a mechanic, the services performed on the car end up as part of measured real GDP, but if you and a friend repair your car, these services are not included in the statistics. The biggest category of do-it-yourself services left out of the official GDP statistics consists of those performed in the house by homemakers. It is widely estimated, for example, that the *weekly* value of a homemaker's services is several hundred dollars, none of which is included in the official figures for real GDP. Then there is the matter of the huge volume of transactions— hundreds of billions of dollars per year—in markets for illegal and underground activities. In some "true" measure of real GDP, we should probably add in these activities, which include prostitution and the illegal drug trade, because such goods and services presumably generate satisfaction to the individuals purchasing them. We should also include "underground" income that is the result of legal activities but is not reported. Some of this income goes unreported by individuals hoping to evade income taxes, but it also includes much of the income earned by illegal immigrants, who do not report their incomes because they do not wish to be deported.

ARE SUBTRACTIONS NECESSARY, TOO?

If we were able to adjust for the items mentioned in the previous section, we might agree that we have a solid measure of real GDP. Nevertheless, we might also feel that we should make some adjustments to real GDP to get a more accurate notion of the level of our material standard of living. For example, the government statisticians treat as equivalent the $5 you spend on gasoline to go on a date in the evening and the $5 you spend on gasoline for your trip to work in the morning. Clearly, however, most people would not think about these two expenditures in the same way.

The next category of items we might focus on is sometimes referred to as "regrettable necessities." This includes diplomacy, national security, police and fire protection, and prison facilities. These items typically don't yield consumer satisfaction in and of themselves. They are produced because they make it possible for us to enjoy the consumption of other goods. In this sense, we can think about regrettable necessities as intermediate goods that go into the production of other goods. As such, they probably should be subtracted from real GDP to get to a better measure of the final goods relevant to individuals, but the government statisticians will not allow it.

It is also important to recognize that our urbanized, industrialized society has some drawbacks. Big cities make large-scale commercial activities (and thus more market goods) feasible, but they also bring with them a variety of urban disamenities, such as congestion, noise, and litter. If we are interested in some measure of welfare, we should make deductions from real GDP for such sources of dissatisfaction. (The same reasoning applies to pollution in general.) It is difficult to put a precise numerical value on them, however, and so none of the official statistics are adjusted.

WHAT DOES GDP TELL US?

At this point you might well be wondering whether real GDP has any link at all to what we might think of as happiness or welfare. After all, if the time you spend tinkering on your classic car is *excluded* from real GDP, while the gas you burn stuck in traffic every morning is *included* in real GDP, it almost seems as though the government accountants have things upside down and backwards. Just as importantly, plenty of the items that are important in our GDP (fast food, for example) are a negligible part of GDP in other countries, while the items that are important to them (say, cassava root) are almost unknown to most of us. What, then, can we learn from comparisons of real GDP across nations? (The same query might be asked about comparisons of different time periods *within* a country. Whale oil was a big deal in 1840, whereas smart phones matter a lot today.)

For many years, economists thought that such comparisons, even though routinely made, might just as routinely mean nothing. Imagine, for example, that economies with much more goods and services were also saddled with much more crime and pollution and much less leisure time. Under these circumstances, real GDP might bear no relationship whatsoever to the welfare, happiness, or satisfaction experienced by different people in different lands, or by people at different points in time in the same country. As it turns out, however, it now appears that real GDP might actually be quite useful in making these comparisons across people and countries, and over time.

BRINGING IN HAPPINESS

Even as economists have been busy measuring real GDP, a variety of other researchers—such as sociologists, psychologists, and political scientists—have been asking people how happy or satisfied they are with their lives. Now, answers to questions such as these always need to be taken with a grain of salt and a dose of caution because "talk is cheap." That is, when you go to the store to buy something, you must make a real sacrifice to obtain the item. But when a person conducting a poll asks you whether you are happy or unhappy, it costs no more to check the box next to "happy" than it does to check the box next to "unhappy."

Keeping this caution in mind, economists Betsey Stevenson and Judson Wolfers thought it might be useful to see if there was any link between measures of real GDP and measures of happiness. Obviously, some adjustments were in order even before beginning. For example, some countries are large and some are small, so the researchers divided real GDP by population in each nation to obtain **real GDP per capita.** Similarly, the exact questions asked of people differed across nations and over time, so considerable work was needed to put all of the answers on a comparable footing. After all of this was done, however, the results were striking.

REAL GDP AND HAPPINESS ARE STRONGLY LINKED

Stevenson and Wolfers found that there is a strong and consistent positive relationship between real GDP per capita and reported levels of happiness. Using data spanning many decades and covering well over one hundred countries, the authors show that when per capita real GDP is higher, reported measures of satisfaction or happiness are higher also. Notably, there is no "satiation" point—that is, it appears that even the richest and happiest peoples have the opportunity to become even happier as their incomes rise further.

The authors examine the data in three different ways. First, they look at measures of income (real GDP per capita) and happiness (or reported well-being) across different people within the same country at one point in time. Then they examine income and well-being across different countries at the same point in time, and finally, they assess real per capita GDP and happiness over long periods of time within given countries. In each case, they observe the same strong positive relationship: People with higher real per capita incomes report being happier.

Obviously, real income is not the only factor that influences happiness. Gender, age, and many difficult-to-measure variables are important also. Moreover, it is entirely possible that some other factor is responsible for simultaneously creating high levels of income and happiness. For example, in Chapter 4 we noted that secure property rights and the rule of law are important in creating high levels of real GDP per capita. It may be true that these same institutions also happen to make people happier, perhaps because they enhance personal liberty. Nevertheless, even if "money can't buy happiness," the results of Stevenson and Wolfers make one point clear: Despite all of its imperfections, real GDP per capita is strongly linked to well-being, at least as perceived by the human beings being asked about such matters. Thus, although GDP may not be a perfect measure of anything, we keep on using it because it seems to beat all of the alternatives.

FOR CRITICAL ANALYSIS

1. How does one determine what is a final good or service and what is a regrettable necessity or an intermediate good? In other words, where does one draw the line?

2. Why is it important to carefully distinguish between GDP and real GDP? Answer the same query for real GDP versus *per capita* real GDP.

3. Would you categorize each of the following expenditures as intermediate goods, regrettable necessities, or consumption goods: (a) a spare tire, (b) surgery to repair a badly broken arm, (c) a Botox injection to remove forehead wrinkles, (d) voice lessons, and (e) expenditures on your college education? Explain your reasoning in each instance. Would your answers to (c) and (d) change if you knew that the purchaser was a professional singer who made many public appearances? Why or why not?

4. Over the past 40 years, growing numbers of women have entered the labor force, becoming employed outside the home. As a result, many women now hire people to do household tasks (such as child-care and house cleaning) that they used to do themselves. What impact does this "hiring out" of household tasks have on measures on GDP? Explain.

5. Over the past 40 years, the levels of water and air pollution in the United States have declined substantially. Would these environmental improvements likely be reflected in reported measures of well-being or happiness? Would they likely be reflected in GDP?

6. Are nations with large underground economies likely to be happier or unhappier than one would expect, given their *measured* levels of real per capita GDP? Explain.

CHAPTER 6

What's in a Word? Plenty, When It's the "R" Word

Incumbent presidents (and members of their political party) hate the "R" word. We speak here of **recession,** a word used to describe a downturn or stagnation in overall, nationwide economic activity. Politicians' attitudes toward recessions are driven by the simple fact that people tend to "vote their pocketbooks." That is, when the economy is doing well, voters are likely to return incumbent politicians to office, but when the economy is doing poorly, voters are likely to "throw the bums out." Interestingly, although *recession* is the word most commonly used to describe a period of poor performance by the economy, most people do not really know what the word means.

THE NBER

Ever since its founding in 1920, a private organization called the National Bureau of Economic Research (NBER) has sought to accurately measure the state of overall economic conditions in the United States. (It also sponsors research on other economic issues.) Over time, the NBER developed a reputation for measuring the economy's performance in an evenhanded and useful way. As a result, most people now accept without argument what the NBER has to say about the state of the economy. Most notably, this means that it is the NBER that we rely on to tell us when we are in a recession.

If you are an avid reader of newspapers, you may have heard a recession defined as any period in which there are at least two quarters (three-month periods) of declining **real gross domestic product (real GDP).** In fact, the NBER's recession-dating committee places little reliance on the performance of real (inflation-adjusted) GDP when deciding on the state of the economy. There are two reasons for this. First, the government measures GDP only on a quarterly basis, and the NBER prefers to focus on more timely data that are available at least monthly. Second, the official GDP numbers are subject to frequent and often substantial revisions, so what once looked like good economic performance might suddenly look bad, and vice versa.

Looking back at 2001 (a turbulent year), for example, the initial figures showed that real GDP declined in only one quarter during the year. But when the government finally finished all of its revisions to the data, it turned out that real GDP actually fell during *three* quarters of 2001. In 2007, the government issued a revision of its revised GDP figures for 2004–2006. Of the twelve quarters covered by this "revision of the revisions," the numbers for all twelve were changed: Two were revised upward and ten downward. The 2011 set of revisions altered virtually every GDP figure for the preceding decade. One can easily see why an organization such as the NBER, which prides itself on reliability and accuracy, might be reluctant to place too much weight on measures of real GDP.

So what does the NBER use as its criteria in measuring a recession? Its official definition gives us some insight: "A recession is a significant decline in activity spread across the economy, lasting more than a few months, visible in industrial production, employment, real income, and wholesale–retail sales." Those are a lot of words to define just one term, but it is not too difficult to get a handle on it. The point to note at the outset is that the NBER focuses chiefly on four separate pieces of information:

- Industrial production
- Employment
- Real income (measured by inflation-adjusted personal income of consumers)
- Sales at both the wholesale and retail levels

All of these figures are reliably available on a monthly basis, and so every month the NBER uses the latest figures on each to take the pulse of the economy. When all four move upward, that is generally good news. When all move downward, that is definitely bad news. And when some move in one direction and some in another direction, that is when expert judgment comes into play.

The Three *D*'s

If the NBER recession-dating committee uses a strict formula to time the onset or end of a recession, the committee members do not reveal what it is. What they do reveal is that they look for three crucial elements, all starting with the letter *D*, when they officially announce the start or end of a recession:

1. *Depth.* If there is a downturn in one or more of the four key variables, the NBER focuses first on the magnitude of that downturn. For example, in an economy like ours with total employment of over 140 million, a drop of 50,000 in employment would not be crucial, but an employment drop of, say, 1 million surely would be considered significant.

2. *Duration.* Month-to-month fluctuations in economic activity are the norm in our economy. These fluctuations occur partly because our measures of economic activity are imperfect and partly because, in an economy as complex as ours, many things are happening all the time that have the capacity to affect the overall performance of the economy. Thus, if real personal income moves up or down for a month or even two months in a row, the recession-dating committee is likely to determine that such a change is well within the bounds of normal variation. If a trend persists for, say, six months, the committee is likely to place a much heavier weight on that movement.

3. *Dispersion.* Because the NBER is trying to measure the overall state of the economy, it wants to make sure that it is not being misled by economic developments that may be important to many people but are not reliable indicators of the overall state of the economy. For example, America is becoming less dependent on industrial production and more reliant on service industries. In addition, it is well known that industrial production is sensitive to sharp movements not shared by sectors elsewhere in the economy. Hence, the NBER tempers the importance of industrial production by simultaneously relying on measures such as wholesale and retail sales to make sure that it has a picture of what is happening throughout the economy.

A PRECISE ANSWER

Having blended its four measures of the economy in a way that reflects its focus on the three *D*'s, the recession-dating committee makes its decision. A recession, in its view, begins "just after the economy reaches a peak of activity" and ends "as the economy reaches its trough" and starts expanding again. Between trough and peak, the economy is said to be in an **expansion.** Historically, the normal state of the economy is expansion. Most recessions are brief (usually ending within 12–18 months), and in recent decades they have been rare. Our most recent recession, coming after six years of economic expansion, began in December 2007 and ended in June 2009.

The four measures used by the NBER to date recessions generally move fairly closely together. Although individually they sometimes give conflicting signals for short periods of time, they soon enough start playing the same song. Nevertheless, some contention about the NBER's decisions remains. There are two sources of debate: One focuses on *potential* growth of economic activity, and the other highlights the importance of population growth.

The NBER defines a recession as an absolute decline in economic activity. Yet some economists note that for the past couple of centuries, growth in economic activity from year to year has been the norm in most developed nations, including the United States. Hence, they argue, a recession should be declared whenever growth falls significantly below its long-term potential. This dispute becomes more important when there is reason to believe that potential growth has shifted for some reason or when comparing the current performance of two nations that are growing at different rates. For example, suppose nation X has potential growth of 4 percent per year while nation Y has potential growth of only 2 percent per year. If both are actually growing at 2 percent, the unemployment rate in X will be rising, and some economists would argue that this fact is sufficient to declare that X is in a state of recession. The biggest problem with this proposed measure of recession is that it is difficult to declare with confidence exactly what the potential growth rate of any country is.

The second point of contention starts with the observation that the population is growing in most countries. Hence, even if economic activity is growing, the well-being of the average citizen might not be. For example, suppose the population is growing 3 percent per year, but real personal income is growing only 2 percent per year. Assuming that the other measures of activity were performing like personal income, the NBER would say the economy was in an expansion phase, even though **real per capita income** was declining. Some economists would argue that this state of affairs should be declared a recession, given that the term is supposed to indicate a less-than-healthy economy. This point has some validity. Nevertheless, there have not been many prolonged periods when the NBER has said the economy was expanding while real per capita income was falling.

Ultimately, of course, even if the recession-dating committee somehow tinkered with its methods to better acknowledge the importance of potential growth and population changes, some other issue would undoubtedly be raised to dispute the NBER's conclusions. For now, most economists are content to rely on the NBER to make the call. Most politicians are, too—except, of course, when it suits them otherwise. As for ordinary voters, well, even if they do not know how a recession is defined, they surely know what one feels like—and are likely to vote accordingly.

For Critical Analysis

1. Why is it important, both for the political process and for our understanding of the economy, for the NBER to resist the temptation to change its definition of a recession to fit the latest political pressures or economic fads?

2. Do you think that voters care more about whether the NBER says the economy is in a state of recession or whether they and their friends and family members are employed in good jobs? Why do politicians make a big deal over whether the economy is "officially" in a recession or an expansion? (*Hint:* Is it hard for the average voter to tell what is going on in the economy outside his or her community, leaving the voter dependent on simple measures—or labels—of what is happening elsewhere in the economy?)

3. Examine the data from the last six recessions. (Good sources for data are www.nber.org/cycles/recessions.html, www.bea.gov, and www.globalindicators.org.) Rank them on the basis of both duration and severity. The first is easy; the second is more difficult: Is it possible that some people—either politicians or other citizens—might disagree about how to measure the severity of a particular recession? How would you measure it?

4. Return to the data you examined for question 3. Some people have called the recession of 2007–2009 the "Great Recession." Based on the data you think most relevant, is this latest recession worthy of being singled out as "Great"? Explain.

5. The stock market has been called a "leading indicator" of future economic activity, while the unemployment rate has been called a "lagging indicator" of past economic activity. Combine the data from questions 3 and 4, including data on the stock market and the unemployment rate to answer the following two questions:

   a. How well do movements in a stock price index (such as the DJIA or the S&P 500) predict ahead of time the beginning or end of each recession?

   b. How well do beginnings or endings of recessions predict future changes, up or down, in the unemployment rate?

6. Why do we bother to declare the beginning or end of something called a "recession"?

CHAPTER 7

The Great Stagflation

From December 2007 until June 2009, the U.S. economy experienced an economic downturn of historic proportions. **Real gross domestic product (real GDP)** fell sharply, housing foreclosures soared, and millions of people lost their jobs.

When the recession ended, however, many people were optimistic about the years ahead. After all, in the United States and elsewhere, major recessions are generally followed by robust economic recoveries. But the recovery that followed the recession of 2007–2009 was anything but robust. In fact, the first four years of recovery were so weak that some observers began referring to that period as the Great Stagflation. Our mission is to see why the recovery from the recession of 2007–2009 was so dismal.

THE GREAT RECESSION

The recession of 2007–2009, sometimes referred to as the Great Recession, was arguably worse than any other we have had since World War II. It also likely ranks among the half dozen or so worst we have had in our history. For example, total employment fell 6 percent, compared to a mere 2 percent in the 2000–2001 recession, and 5 percent in 1948–1949, which had previously been the largest postwar drop. Similarly, total output in the economy fell 4.8 percent in 2007–2009. The largest prior decline in a postwar recession was the 3.2 percent fall in 1973–1974. In addition, although the unemployment rate (10 percent) did not get as high as it had in the 1981–1982 recession (10.8 percent), the jump in the unemployment rate was similar in both recessions—just over five percentage points.

Of course, while the recession of 2007–2009 was large compared to other postwar recessions, it was minor compared to the Great Depression (1929–1933) and modest compared to the recessions of 1919–1920 and 1937–1938. Nonetheless, the latest recession will likely stick with the American people for a long time, for two well-deserved reasons. First, most economists agree that if the Federal Reserve had not stepped in aggressively to end the financial panic of 2008, the consequences could have rivaled those experienced in 1929–1933 when output fell 30 percent and the unemployment rate hit 25 percent. Second, the housing market was utterly devastated in the recession of 2007–2009, to a degree not seen since the 1930s. Housing prices fell over 30 percent, and millions of families lost their homes. The number of housing starts, which had previously peaked at 2 million per year, plunged to under 500,000. In many communities, housing constructions ground to a complete halt, often with houses simply left behind, partially finished. All in all, there is no doubt that the recession of 2007–2009 was severe.

RECESSION AND RECOVERY

A recession is a time when the economy is, by definition, not in long-run equilibrium. Business in all markets is disrupted—meaning that there is plenty of mutually beneficial exchange that should be occurring, but is not. Workers and business owners all have strong incentive to get back to work and back to business as usual, and the further they have been pushed away from equilibrium, the greater are those incentives. As a result, there is a general rule that applies to recessions and the recoveries that follow them: The deeper the recession, the stronger the recovery.

If we look at the relatively mild recessions of 1990–1991 and 2001, we see that during the four years after each of them, real GDP grew at an average pace of about 3.1 percent per year. During the four years after the much deeper recession of 1981–1982, real GDP roared back at an average rate of 5.1 percent per year. If we go back to the worst of the all, the Great Depression, the results are even more dramatic. During the first four years after the Great Depression ended, real GDP grew at a torrid 9.0 percent per year.

Based on these numbers, we would surely expect that the Great Recession would have been followed by a robust recovery, perhaps similar to the strong recovery after the recession of 1981–1982. In fact, this did not happen. Indeed, during the first four years after the end of the 2007–2009 recession, real GDP grew an average of only about 2.5 percent per year. This was not merely significantly slower than the typical economic recovery. It did not even reach the 3.1 percent average growth in GDP that the United States has experienced since World War II. (And remember, this 3.1 percent rate includes both recessions and recoveries.) In short, the initial recovery from the Great Recession fell flat.

The Great Stagflation

While there is no universally agreed-upon definition of a **stagflation**, most economists take it to mean a period of macroeconomic stagnation, plus **inflation**. It is a stretch of time in which there is lackluster performance in the overall economy, accompanied by rising prices of goods and services. The fact that real GDP growth during 2009–2013 failed to match up with average post–World War II performance is part of the story. Another part is that the inflation rate during the four years after the recession averaged about 2.5 percent per year, which is above the Federal Reserve System's target rate of 2.0 percent per year.

There are other macroeconomic measures that also suggest that recovery from the 2007–2009 recession was weak. It took more than three years, for example, for the unemployment rate to inch down from 10 to 8 percent. Investment spending, which is normally a big force in economic recoveries, grew far more slowly than it normally does. Consumer confidence, which leapt by more than 50 percent in the 12 months after the end of the 1981–1982 recession, spent the first three *years* going sideways after the Great Recession. By 2013, it was clear that recovery was anemic.

Housing

Normally, new home construction is one of the first economic activities that accelerate in the aftermath of recession. Typically interest rates have fallen during the recession, and when the downturn ends, consumer confidence normally rises rapidly. The combination typically spurs a surge in the demand for new homes. Not so in the initial aftermath of 2007–2009, for reasons that go back to the period preceding the recession.

During the years 2001–2006, a variety of federal policies encouraged substantial overbuilding, particularly of single-family houses and condominiums. Home ownership soared to record levels. This seemed like a good thing, until the recession hit and the housing market collapsed. Federal policies, it turned out, had helped encourage people to buy houses even if their incomes did not justify those purchases. When the economy soured, many of those people simply walked away from their homes, and many more struggled to stay in them, in the face of daunting mortgage payments.

Foreclosures swept across the country, and in Arizona, Florida, Nevada, and parts of California, some neighborhoods became virtual ghost towns as people were forced out of their homes—or moved out shortly before the bank showed up to evict them. Simply put, at existing prices, housing in the United States was overbuilt—there was an **excess supply** of housing. The market response was just what you would expect: House prices plunged by more than 30 percent nationwide and 50 percent or more in some of the hardest-hit areas. Gradually, the excess supply cleared, but the adjustment process was measured in years, not months.

New home construction, which had reached 2 million units in 2005, plunged to barely one-quarter of that by 2009. Indeed, between its peak at the end of 2005 and its trough in the spring of 2009, home construction fell 75 percent, but instead of recovering sharply at the end of the recession, home construction edged up only slowly and slightly for the first three years and more. Potential new homes were competing with millions of empty existing homes across the country. Moreover, home prices were still falling, even as the overall price level was rising. So builders did not build, did not hire workers, and did not buy construction materials. Thus, the unemployed former construction workers did not spend much on goods and services, nor did the people who used to work for companies that made construction equipment and materials. Instead of buoying the economy, housing was weighing it down.

THE ECONOMIC SAFETY NET

Government programs that comprise the so-called **economic safety net** include unemployment insurance, welfare, and food stamps. Spending on these programs rises automatically during recessions, as unemployment rises and people's reliance on **cash and noncash transfers** goes up. Normally, these programs help bolster consumer spending in downturns and thus help moderate recessions. Although such transfers performed this function in 2007–2009, changes in these programs actually *impeded* the recovery from the recession.

To see how, let's consider the following changes:

- *Unemployment benefits*—These payments by the federal and state governments to the unemployed normally can be collected for a maximum of twenty-six weeks (about six months). During this recession, however, Congress increased the maximum collection period to ninety-nine weeks (that is almost two full years). This surely helped ease the pain of unemployment. Nevertheless, it is well known that unemployment benefits slow people's transition from unemployment to employment. (For example, the single best predictor of when an unemployed person will return to work is the expiration of his or her unemployment benefits.) By lengthening the eligibility period for benefits to a record duration, Congress reduced incentives for people to find new jobs. This helped keep the unemployment rate high for a longer-than-normal period. It also likely dampened overall spending during the recovery phase, because people's unemployment benefits were lower than the wages they would have earned once reemployed.

The extended eligibility for unemployment benefits was accompanied by an increase in the dollar amount of those benefits. In addition, for the first time, many people who were unemployed could have most of their health insurance premiums paid by the federal government. Whatever the merits of these higher benefits and insurance subsidies, there is little doubt that they reduced incentives for people to get back to work promptly and thereby helped slow recovery from the recession.

- *Welfare*—Officially called Temporary Assistance to Needy Families (TANF), this program provides for cash payments to low-income families, especially when one or more adults in a family are unemployed. In 1997 President Clinton strengthened the incentives for TANF recipients to return to work quickly. Under President Obama, however, these incentives were weakened. Once the recession ended in June 2009, Obama's policy change helped keep the unemployment rate higher than it would have been. It also likely dampened overall spending, because people's welfare benefits were lower than the wages they would have earned once reemployed.

- *Food stamps*—These are government-issued **vouchers** that can be used by low-income people to pay for eligible food items. (They got their name because they used to be issued in booklets much like postage stamps. These days people typically receive electronic transfers to debit cards.) Under President Obama, eligibility rules for receipt of benefits were loosened considerably, and monthly benefits increased. Combined with the recession, these changes caused the number of people on food stamps to soar. There were particularly large increases in the number of able-bodied adults on food stamps. Just as with unemployment benefits and welfare, such policy changes prolong unemployment, because food stamp recipients could lose their benefits if they got jobs. The benefits make them better off, but their incomes are lower than if they worked, which has likely reduced postrecession economic growth.

Government Spending and the Specter of Higher Taxes

Under both President Bush and President Obama, federal spending rose sharply during the recession. In Chapter 13 we discuss the extent to which this spending might have stimulated the economy. Here we focus on the dark side of that spending—the fact that it must be paid for with taxes.

These new taxes may come sooner or they may come later, but come they must, and the specter of these taxes must invariably dampen both business and consumer spending. Corporate profit taxes reduce the after-tax return to investment and thus cause investment spending to fall. Personal income taxes reduce disposable income and also the incentive for people to work. On both counts, personal income and consumption spending will be lower. The combined decline in investment and consumption spending reduces **aggregate demand** and employment, thereby slowing economic recovery.

As we note in Chapter 13, the "stimulus" spending that preceded these taxes may well have softened the recession. Nonetheless, as soon as the piper must be paid—that is, after the recession—the specter and reality of higher taxes kick in. The result is a less robust recovery. In the case of 2009–2013, this problem was likely made worse because of the inability of Congress and the president to agree on exactly *who* would pay the higher taxes. This heightened uncertainty made investment by both firms and individuals riskier than it would have been had tax bills been known. This, in turn, surely reduced investment even further and thus prolonged economic stagnation.

Regulation and More Regulation

It is usually police and military actions that grab the headlines in both the war on drugs and the war on terror, but both wars have been accompanied by a barrage of new regulations over the last dozen years or so. Under President Bush and President Obama, regulations on financial institutions, the transportation industry, and education have imposed serious and costly new burdens across the economy. And since the Panic of 2008, an entirely new layer of financial regulations is now being termed the "war on borrowing," because the regulations have made it so difficult for anyone to borrow funds for any purpose.

During the strong economic times of 2001–2007, the costs and rigidities associated with new regulations were largely masked by the healthy economy, but once the recession hit, their adverse effects became clear. This burden has recently intensified due to large-scale new environmental and health care regulations, which the Obama Administration deferred until after the election of 2012. Costs and uncertainty have risen, and investment and consumption spending have suffered. The result has been a drag on the economy.

THE FUTURE

Some of the policies we have discussed in this chapter helped ease the blow of the Great Recession. Others surely yielded benefits by reducing the flow of money from drug smuggling or protecting Americans from terrorists, pollution, or inadequate health care insurance. But there is no free lunch. There is a cost to every action, and for the policies discussed here, part of those costs have come in the form of prolonged high unemployment, sluggish real growth, and economic stagnation. It is a lesson we ignore at our peril.

FOR CRITICAL ANALYSIS

1. Spending on the food stamp program doubled during the first Obama Administration, reaching $82 billion per year. People who received additional aid under the program surely benefitted from it, but people who had to pay for the program just as surely were made worse off. On what basis would you decide how much we should spend on food stamps? Why don't we simply have food stamps for everyone?

2. Under President Clinton's added work requirements, many long-term welfare recipients got jobs. Moreover, there is evidence that the educational performance of the children of these parents improved substantially. Why do you suppose that President Obama decided to effectively dismantle the reforms that President Clinton had worked so hard to achieve?

3. In this question, consider only the eighteen months for which the latest recession lasted. Suppose that the liberalization of unemployment benefits tended to *raise* the unemployment rate because it reduced the incentive of the unemployed to return to work. How would you decide whether the liberalization of benefits was good or bad for the economy?

4. Now look at the four years *after* the recession and again answer the query posed in question 3. Is the impact on the unemployment

rate the only factor to consider? (If you think other factors should be considered, make sure that you take into account both the disadvantages and the advantages of liberalized benefits.)

5. If higher federal spending reduces the unemployment rate, why don't we increase federal spending until the unemployment rate is 3 or 4 percent?

6. As a practical matter, when Congress created the Environmental Protection Agency (EPA), it required the agency to *ignore* economic costs when deciding what regulations to issue. Analyze how this requirement changes the likelihood that the EPA issues regulations that make life better for Americans.

CHAPTER **8**

The Case of the Disappearing Workers

Every month, the Bureau of Labor Statistics (BLS) goes out into the labor market to determine how many unemployed people there are in the United States. With the data it acquires, the BLS calculates the **unemployment rate.** This number is a key indication of how well the economy is doing. The unemployment rate is calculated in a seemingly straightforward way: It is the percentage of the total **labor force** that is (i) aged 16 and older but not institutionalized or in school, and (ii) actively seeking employment but has not found it.

The reelection chances of incumbent presidents often hinge on the estimated rate of unemployment. Historically, when the unemployment rate is rising, the president's chances of reelection have been far worse than when the rate is stable or falling. As the old saying goes, "people vote their pocketbooks" (or in this case, their pay stubs).

For this and a variety of other reasons, understanding how the unemployment rate is measured is important for politicians and ordinary citizens alike. Remarkably, however, there is little consensus about the accuracy of unemployment statistics in the United States. First, consider the period when the United States had its highest measured rate of unemployment—the Great Depression, which started in 1929 and did not fully end until a decade later.

Twenty-Five Percent Unemployment— Hard to Imagine

If you look at official government statistics on the unemployment rate during the Great Depression, you will find that in some statistical series, the rate hit 25 percent—meaning that one of every four Americans who were part of the labor force could not find a job during the depth of the depression. That high unemployment rate, of course, makes any **recession** since then seem insignificant in terms of the proportion of people adversely affected.

Some economists, though, are not so sure that one-fourth of the labor force was actually unemployed during the Great Depression. The reason is simple: At that time, the federal government had instituted numerous programs to "put people back to work." These included the Works Progress Administration (WPA), the Civilian Conservation Corps (CCC), and various lesser programs. Government statisticians decided that everyone working in these federally sponsored "make-work" programs would have been unemployed otherwise. Consequently, they decided to count these millions of Americans as unemployed. Michael Darby, an economist at UCLA, subsequently recalculated unemployment statistics for the depth of the Great Depression. After adjusting for people who were actually working but were counted as unemployed, he found a maximum unemployment rate of 17 percent. This number is still the highest we have had in modern times, but it is certainly not one-fourth of the labor force.

How much sense does Darby's adjustment make? The argument against the official government statistics is straightforward: The federal government taxed individuals and businesses to pay workers at the WPA and CCC. Had the federal government not levied the taxes to pay these new government employees, the private sector would have had more disposable income, more spending, and higher employment. Whether all of those people would have gotten private-sector jobs is impossible to know, but it is clear that the official numbers greatly overstated the true unemployment rate during the Great Depression.

Discouraged Workers: A Cover for a Higher "True" Unemployment Rate?

Certain individuals, after spending some time in the pool of the unemployed, may become discouraged about their future job prospects. They may leave the labor market to go back to school, to retire, to work full time at home without pay, or just to take some time off. Whichever path they choose, when interviewers from the BLS ask these individuals whether they are "actively looking for a job," they say no. Individuals such as these are often referred to as **discouraged workers.** They might seek work if labor market conditions were better and potential wages were higher, but they have decided that such is not the case, so they have left the labor market. For years, some critics of the officially measured unemployment rate have argued that during recessions, the rising numbers of discouraged workers cause the government to grossly underestimate the actual rate of unemployment.

To get a feel for the labor market numbers, let's look at the 1990s, perhaps one of the greatest periods of rising employment in U.S. history. During that decade an additional 18 million people became employed, while the unemployment rate fell to 4 percent. Moreover, far fewer workers settled for part-time jobs. Many who had been retired came back to work, and many of those about to retire continued to work. There were even large numbers of students who left school to take high-paying jobs in the technology sector.

The onset of the 2001 recession produced a turnaround in all of those statistics. The number of unemployed rose by about 3 million individuals. The number of part-time workers who indicated that they would like to work full time rose by over a million, and the proportion of those out of work for more than half a year increased by over 50 percent.

According to some economists, another 2 million workers dropped out of the labor force—the so-called discouraged-worker problem. For example, University of Chicago economist Robert Topel claims, "The unemployment rate does not mean what it did 20 years ago." He argues that employment opportunities for the least skilled workers no longer exist in today's labor market, so such individuals simply left the labor force, discouraged and forgotten by the statisticians who compile the official numbers.

ARE DISCOURAGED WORKERS A PROBLEM?

Other economists argue differently. They note that the labor market is no different from any other market, so we can analyze it just as we analyze the market for any other good or service. The **labor supply curve** is upward-sloping. That means that as overall wages rise (corrected for inflation, of course), the quantity of labor supplied would be expected to increase. After all, when the inflation-corrected price of just about anything else goes up, we observe that the quantity supplied goes up, too. Therefore, argue these economists, the concept of discouraged workers is basically flawed. They say it makes no more sense to talk of discouraged workers than it would to talk of "discouraged apples" that are no longer offered for sale when the price of apples falls.

Because of the upward-sloping supply curve of labor, when **real wages** rise economy-wide, we expect that retirees and those about to retire will return to or remain in the labor market. We expect students to quit school early if the wages they can earn are relatively high. The opposite must occur when we go into a recession or the economy stagnates. That is, with reduced wage growth (or even declines in economywide real wages) and reduced employment opportunities, we expect more young people to stay in school longer, retirees to stay retired, and those about to retire to actually do so. In other words, we expect the same behavior in response to incentives that we observe in all other markets.

DISABILITY INSURANCE AND
LABOR FORCE PARTICIPATION

It is also worth noting that some, perhaps many, of the departures from the labor force by low-skill individuals may actually be prompted by certain government programs. We refer here to a portion of the Social Security program that has expanded dramatically over the past 20 years. It involves **disability payments.** Originally established in 1956 as a program to help individuals under age 65 who are truly disabled, Social Security Disability Insurance (SSDI) has become the federal government's second fastest growing program (after Medicare). The real value of benefits has steadily risen and the Social Security Administration (SSA) has gradually made it easier for individuals to meet the legal criteria for "disabled" status. SSDI now accounts for over $125 billion in federal spending per year. Under SSDI, even individuals who are not truly disabled can receive payments from the government when they do not work.

In addition, because Social Security also offers Supplemental Security Income (SSI) payments for disabled people who have little or no track record in the labor force, some people are calling disability insurance the centerpiece of a new U.S. welfare state. Since 1990, the number of people receiving disability payments from the SSA has soared to over 14 million—perhaps not surprising when you consider that the real value of the monthly benefits a person can collect has risen almost 60 percent in the past thirty-five years. The federal government now spends more on disability payments than on food stamps or unemployment benefits.

What does this mean? Simply that people who might have worked through chronic pain or temporary injuries—particularly those without extensive training and education—have chosen to receive a government disability benefit instead. The average Social Security disability payment is over $1,100 per month, tax-free. For many on the lower rungs of the job ladder, $1,100 per month tax-free seems pretty good. Indeed, those receiving disability payments make up the largest group of the 2 million or so who left the labor force during the 2001–2002 recession. Preliminary estimates suggest that the same pattern held true for the recession of 2007–2009. And because people respond to incentives, we can be sure of one thing: Whatever happens to the economy in the future, if the real value of disability payments keeps rising, so will the number of people with disabilities.

FOR CRITICAL ANALYSIS

1. To what extent do you believe that the existence of unemployment benefits increases the duration of unemployment and consequently the unemployment rate? (*Hint:* Use demand analysis and **opportunity cost.**)

2. Is it possible for the unemployment rate to be "too low"? In other words, can you conceive of a situation in which the economy would be worse off in the long run because there is not enough unemployment?

3. It is believed that much of the increase in the number of people collecting SSDI has resulted from decisions by workers at the SSA to make it easier to qualify for benefits. How are the disability rules set by SSA workers likely to change depending on (i) whether the SSA budget is held constant or expands when the number of SSDI recipients rises, (ii) the overall state of the economy, especially the unemployment rate, and (iii) the likelihood that individuals with disabilities will be discriminated against in the workplace?

4. What would happen to the number of disabled people if Social Security disability payments were made subject to income taxes? Explain.

5. During the latest recession Congress increased the length of time people could receive unemployment benefits to ninety-nine weeks (almost two years) from its previous level of twenty-six weeks (about six months). Analyze the impact of this change on (i) the unemployment rate and (ii) the average duration of unemployment.

6. Imagine that at two different times—late 1933 (when the economy was struggling out of the depths of the Depression) and late 1939 (when the economy was expanding rapidly)—there were a million people on make-work government jobs who were officially classified as "unemployed." In which year (1933 or 1939) were these make-work employees more likely to have been displaced from private-sector jobs and in which were they more likely to have been displaced from the ranks of the unemployed? Explain. How would this distinction factor into your thinking about whether such people should be officially classed as "employed" or "unemployed"?

CHAPTER 9

Poverty, Wealth, and Equality

In 1960, the poorest 20 percent of households in the United States received a bit over 4 percent of total income. Today, after half a century of government efforts to relieve poverty, the bottom 20 percent receive a bit less than 4 percent of total income. About 40 million Americans lived in poverty in 1960. About 40 million U.S. citizens *still* live in poverty, despite the expenditure of hundreds of billions of dollars in aid for the poor. In the world's richest country, poverty seems remarkably resilient.

FIRST, THE FACTS

If we are to understand why, we must begin by getting the facts straight. First, even though the *absolute* number of Americans living in poverty has not diminished over the past half-century, population growth has brought a sizable reduction in the *proportion* of Americans who are impoverished. As conventionally measured, more than 22 percent of Americans lived in poverty in 1960. Today, as we emerge from one of the worst recessions of our recent history, about 15 percent of the population is below the official poverty line.

Second, over the past 50 years, the **poverty line** has been adjusted upward faster than the cost of living has risen. Hence the *real* standard of living of a family at the poverty line has risen by 50 percent over this period. In contrast, the real standard of living of a family in the middle of the income distribution has risen less than 20 percent over these years. Hence, the people who are counted as poor today are much better off compared to the middle class than they were 50 years ago.

Third, traditional methods of measuring poverty may be misleading because they focus solely on the *cash incomes* of individuals. In effect, government statisticians compute a "minimum adequate" budget for families of various sizes—the "poverty line"—and then determine how many people have cash incomes below this line. Yet major components of the federal government's antipoverty efforts come in the form of **in-kind transfers** (transfers of goods and services, rather than cash) such as Medicare, Medicaid, subsidized housing, food stamps, and school lunches. When the dollar value of these in-kind transfers is included in measures of *total* income, the **standard of living** of persons at lower income levels has improved even more substantially over the years.

There is disagreement over how much of these in-kind transfers should be included in measures of the total income of recipients.[1] Nevertheless, most observers agree that these transfers, plus the **Earned Income Tax Credit** (which gives special **tax rebates** to low-income individuals), are major sources of income for people at the bottom of the income distribution. Adjusting for these transfers and tax credits, it seems likely that over the past fifty years, the proportion of Americans living below the poverty line has been cut roughly in half. Just as important, the real standard of living for the poorest 20 percent of the population has doubled since the mid-1960s. In short, the incidence of poverty in this country has declined markedly over the past half-century, and individuals who remain officially classified as "poor" have a far higher real standard of living than the poor of the 1960s.

The Impact of Income Mobility

Whatever measure of income we use, it is crucial to remember that most Americans exhibit a great deal of **income mobility,** tending to move around in the income distribution over time. The most important source of income mobility is the "life-cycle" pattern of earnings. New entrants to the workforce tend to have lower incomes at first, but most workers can enjoy rising incomes as they gain experience on the job. Typically, annual earnings for an individual reach a maximum at about age 55. Because peak earnings occur well beyond the **median age** of the population (now about age 37), a "snapshot" of the current distribution of

---

1 There are two reasons for this disagreement. First, a given dollar amount of in-kind transfers is generally less valuable than the same dollar amount of cash income because cash offers the recipient a greater amount of choice in his or her consumption pattern. Second, medical care is an important in-kind transfer to the poor. Inclusion of all Medicaid expenditures for the poor would imply that the sicker the poor got, the richer they would be. Presumably, a correct measure would include only those medical expenses that the poor would have to incur if they were *not* poor and so had to pay for the medical care (or medical insurance) out of their own pockets.

earnings will find most individuals "on the way up" toward a higher position in the income distribution. People who have low earnings now are likely, on average, to have higher earnings in the future.

Another major source of income mobility stems from the operation of Lady Luck. At any point in time, the income of high-income people is likely to be abnormally high (relative to what they can expect on average) due to recent good luck—say, because they just won the lottery or just received a bonus at work. Conversely, the income of people who currently have low incomes is likely to be abnormally low due to recent bad luck—for example, because they are laid up after an automobile accident or have become temporarily unemployed. Over time, the effects of Lady Luck tend to average out across the population. Accordingly, people with high income today will tend to have lower income in the future, while people with low income today will tend to have higher future income. Equivalently, many people living below the poverty line are there temporarily rather than permanently.

The importance of income mobility is strikingly revealed in studies examining the incomes of individuals over time. During the 1970s and 1980s, for example, among the people who were in the top 20 percent (quintile) of income earners at the beginning of the decade, fewer than half were in the top quintile by the end of the decade. Similarly, among the people who were in the bottom quintile at the beginning of the decade, almost half had moved out of that bracket by the end of the decade. Despite news stories that suggest otherwise, income mobility remains robust. From 1996 to 2005 (the decade most recently studied), *more than half* of the people who were in the bottom 20 percent income bracket in 1996 had moved out of that bracket by 2005. In addition, almost one-third of the people in the top 20 percent in 1996 had moved (down) out of that bracket by 2005.

Appearances versus Reality

Notwithstanding the data just cited, several forces have either increased income inequality in the United States or given the appearance of such an increase, so it is best to be clear about these. Consider first that a rising proportion of the population is *far* above the poverty line. In 1969, for example, about 4 percent of all people in the United States had earnings six times greater than the poverty-line level. Today, about 6 percent of Americans have earnings that high (above $150,000 for a family of four). Much of this jump in incomes at the top of the income distribution has come at the very top. Thirty years ago, for example, people in the top 10 percent of earners in the United States pulled in about 30 percent of total income. Today, they garner 36 percent. In even more rarified company, the top 1 percent of earners used to account for 9 percent of total income. Today, they take in 14 percent of income. Thus, even though inflation-adjusted incomes are rising across the board, they appear to be rising the fastest at the very top. Economists are seeking to explain this pattern, which first became apparent during the 1990s. Much work remains to be done, but a few answers are emerging.

First, some key demographic changes are occurring in the United States. The nation is aging, and an older population tends to have more income inequality than a young population because older people have had more time to experience rising or falling fortunes. Americans are also becoming better educated, and this tends to increase income inequality. People with little education have incomes that tend to cluster together, while the incomes of well-educated people spread out: Some choose to convert their **human capital** into much higher incomes, while others convert it into added leisure time. Taken together, these two demographic changes, aging and education, can account for more than 75 percent of the *appearance* of greater income inequality.

Second, a substantial part of the rapid income growth at the top has really been a matter of accounting fiction rather than reality. Until the late 1980s, there were substantial tax advantages for the very wealthy to have a large portion of their incomes counted as corporate income rather than personal income. In effect, a big chunk of income for the wealthy used to be hidden—not from the tax authorities but from the policymakers who worry about the distribution of income. Subsequent changes in the tax laws have since encouraged people to report this income as personal rather than corporate. Their true incomes have not really changed; it just looks to policymakers like they have.

The third factor we need to account for is the difference in consumption bundles of those near the top of the income distribution and those near the bottom. High-income individuals tend to spend a larger proportion of their incomes on labor-intensive services (such as investment advice, personal care, and domestic help). Low-income individuals tend to spend a larger share of their incomes on nondurable goods, such as food, clothing, shoes, and toiletries. As it turns out, over the past twenty-five years, the items consumed by lower-income individuals have fallen markedly in cost relative to those consumed by the wealthy. Rising **real wages** have pushed up the costs of service-intensive consumption, while growing international trade with China, India, and other developing nations has pushed down the relative costs of items important to low-income individuals. Overall, this difference in **inflation** rates between the people at the top and those at the bottom of the income distribution has effectively wiped out *all* of the seeming change in their relative incomes over this period.

LIFE AT THE BOTTOM

Nevertheless, it is clear that many people at the bottom of the income distribution are struggling, so we need to take a look at what is going on here. One point is clear: Between 1990 and 2007, the United States experienced a huge influx of immigrants. Newcomers typically earn far less than long-term residents. When large numbers of them are added to the mix of people whose incomes are being measured, *average* income can fall, even when the incomes of all individuals are rising. Thus, immigration has created downward pressure on *measured* incomes at the bottom of the distribution. But new immigrants have also added to competitive pressures in labor markets for less skilled individuals. On balance, it appears that immigration has probably lowered the wages of high school dropouts in the United States by 4–8 percent. (Although this seems small, remember that it is occurring among people whose incomes are already low.) Both these effects have lessened substantially due to the recession of 2007–2009, because deteriorating economic conditions in the United States caused many recent immigrants to return to their homelands.

Public policy has also taken its toll on the incomes of people at the bottom. The war on drugs, for example, has saddled millions of individuals with criminal records, and the impact has been disproportionately greatest on African Americans, whose incomes were lower to begin with. For example, since 1990, more than 2 million African American males have served time in jail on serious (felony) drug charges. Once they return to the workforce, they find that their felony records exclude them from a great many jobs—and not just jobs at the top. Often, convicted felons cannot find positions that pay more than $8 per hour. The result is that the incomes of such individuals are sharply diminished, which means more poverty.

One recent bright spot on the poverty policy front is quickly being extinguished. We refer to the "welfare reform" program begun in 1996 under the leadership of President Clinton. Previously, low-income families had been eligible to receive—for an unlimited duration—federal payments called Aid to Families with Dependent Children (AFDC). The program was converted in 1996 into Temporary Assistance to Needy Families (TANF). Limits were placed on the length of time individuals could receive payments, and all recipients were given additional incentives and assistance to enhance their job skills and to enter or reenter the

labor force. Studies of the impact of this policy change suggest that it modestly raised incomes among those at the bottom of the income distribution. President Obama has chosen to effectively reverse many of the Clinton's reforms, a decision that will most likely lower the standard of living for those at the bottom of the income distribution.

POVERTY HERE AND THERE

Although the resilience of poverty in the United States is discouraging to the poor and to those who study their plight, it is useful to consider these issues in an international context. In other industrialized nations, such as Japan and most countries in Europe, people at the bottom of the income distribution sometimes (but not always) fare better than the poor in the United States. Although the poor typically receive a somewhat larger *share* of national income than in the United States, the national income they share is lower. Hence, compared to the United States, the poorest 10 percent of the population has a higher average income in Japan and Germany but a lower average income in the United Kingdom and Italy.

In developing nations—which is to say, for the vast majority of people around the world—poverty has a completely different meaning than it does in the United States. In Africa and much of Asia, for example, it is commonplace for people at the bottom of the income distribution to be living on the equivalent of $500 per *year* or less—in contrast to the $10,000–$15,000 per year they would earn in the United States. As you saw in Chapter 3, this staggering difference in living standards is due to the vast differences in legal and economic **institutions** that are observed around the world. In the United States, as in many other industrialized nations, these institutions give people the incentives to put their talents to work, and they also protect the fruits of their labors from expropriation by the government. Thus, the best antipoverty program anyone has ever seen is the creation of an institutional environment in which human beings are able to make maximum use of the talents with which they are endowed.

FOR CRITICAL ANALYSIS

1. Why do most modern societies try to reduce poverty? Why don't they do so by simply passing a law that requires that everybody have the same income?

2. How do the "rules of the game" help determine who will be poor and who will not? (*Hint:* How did the Civil Rights Act of 1964, which forbade discrimination on the basis of race, likely affect the

incomes of African Americans compared to the incomes of white Americans?) Explain your answer.

3. Which of the following possible in-kind transfers do you think raises the "true" incomes of recipients the most: (i) free golf lessons, (ii) free transportation on public buses, or (iii) free food? Why?

4. Consider three alternative ways of helping poor people obtain better housing: (i) government-subsidized housing that costs $6,000 per year, (ii) a housing **voucher** worth $6,000 per year toward rent on an apartment or a house, or (iii) $6,000 per year in cash. Which would you prefer if you were poor? On what grounds might you make your decision?

5. How do government programs that provide benefits for the poor (such as food stamps and subsidized housing) change the incentives of people to be classified as "poor"? Explain.

6. One effect of the **minimum wage** is to reduce employment opportunities for minority teenagers. What effect do you think this has on the long-run poverty rate among minorities? Explain.

CHAPTER **10**

Inflation and the Debt Bomb

When George W. Bush took office on January 20, 2001 as president of the United States, the federal government was $5.7 trillion in debt. Over the next eight years, President Bush (with the help of Congress, of course) managed to rack up an *additional* $4.9 trillion in debt on your behalf. Many people were stunned that so much debt could be accumulated so fast. As it turns out, President Bush's spending habits were modest compared to those of President Obama, who took only three years and two months to pile up this much extra debt for you to pay off. Put somewhat differently, approximately 70 percent of *all* of the debt incurred by the United States government since George Washington first took office has been incurred since George W. Bush first took office. The result, as one commentator has put it, is a "debt bomb."

THE DEBT MUST BE PAID

You might say, "what's the big deal?" Indeed, many people think that the government can simply pay off the **national debt** by borrowing more. But it cannot. As we saw in Chapter 4, the ability to borrow does not change the fundamental **budget constraint** facing our society. What is spent today must be paid for now or in the future. And when it is government doing the spending, that higher spending today *must* eventually be matched with higher taxes. Because the record-breaking spending by the federal government over the years 2001–2013 was not matched by higher taxes at the time of the spending, the result was the huge increase in the national debt. But all of that debt means higher taxes (and lower private spending) for you and everyone else who earns income in the United States.

Now, this does not settle what form those higher taxes will take. They might be higher personal income taxes, or higher payroll taxes, or higher corporate taxes, or even higher taxes on estates—the wealth that people leave to their heirs. In fact, almost surely *all* of these taxes will be higher in the future. But there is one other tax that is equally sure to rise in the future. It is called the **inflation tax.**

THE INFLATION TAX

Inflation is a rise in the average level of the prices of goods and services, as measured in terms of a country's **unit of account.** In the United States, the unit of account—that is, the unit in which we express prices—is the dollar. In much of Europe the unit of account is the euro. In Japan it is the yen. In China it is the renminbi, and so forth. But whatever the unit in which prices are measured, when the average level of those prices rise, we call that inflation.

Now, suppose you have a $100 bill stashed in your drawer for emergencies. Further suppose that there is inflation of 10 percent. That is, the price level rises by 10 percent this year. That $100 will buy fewer goods and services than before, because their dollar prices are higher. In this example, the $100 will now buy what it used to take only $90 to acquire. What happened to the other $10? Well, it went to the U.S. government, because it has the ultimate responsibility for the currency it issues. When the purchasing power of the $100 fell by 10 percent this year, so did government's responsibility to you. The 10 percent inflation was a tax of $10 that was just as effective as any other tax would be in transferring wealth from you to the federal government.

ASSETS SUBJECT TO THE INFLATION TAX

The 10 percent tax that was applied to your $100 was at the same time applied to every other piece of currency issued by the U.S. government. Given that there is over $1.1 trillion in U.S. currency in circulation, a 10 percent inflation during the year would effectively impose a tax of $110 billion (= 10 percent × $1.1 trillion) on the holders of currency. Note that these extra taxes would be imposed and collected without the president having to ask for higher taxes and without members of Congress having to vote for those higher taxes. Hence, neither the president nor the Congress has to take responsibility for the new taxes.

It is not just currency that is subject to the inflation tax. Every I.O.U., or debt, of the federal government that is fixed in nominal (or dollar) terms is equally at risk of having this tax applied to it. Thus, mostly as a result of the huge budget deficits racked up by George W. Bush and Barack Obama, the national debt of the United States is today approximately $17 trillion. Of this amount, about $11 trillion is specified in dollar terms and is owned by the "public"—a term that includes not only Aunt Millie (who owns a few savings bonds) but also China (which owns about $1 trillion in federal debt).[1] In our example, a 10 percent inflation would constitute a tax of $1.1 *trillion* on the holders of those $11 trillion in bonds. By anyone's standards, this is a fairly sizable chunk of tax revenues—all collected without the Internal Revenue Service having to lift a finger.

THE TEMPTATION OF INFLATION

At this point, you should begin to see something that just about every government since the beginning of recorded time has seen: When a government has liabilities (such as currency or government bonds) that are fixed in **nominal** terms, inflation is a simple way to increase taxes. Consider, for example, the squabbles among politicians during 2012 about whether federal income taxes on the wealthiest Americans should be raised. At stake were proposed tax hikes that would generate $50 billion a year in extra tax revenue. The battle went on for months, dominating headlines. It played a significant role in the 2012 election and then resumed as soon as the election was over. In January 2013 Congress actually ended up hitting only the upper echelon of the rich with higher income taxes. The result will likely be extra annual tax revenues of no more than $30 billion—which amounts to a few *days'* worth of federal spending.

This same $30 billion per year in additional tax revenues could have been raised, quietly and with no legislation required, if the federal government had been able to engineer an annual inflation rate that was higher by about one-quarter of one percentage point. To put things slightly differently, because the inflation rate in 2012 was about 2.5 percent, the federal government collected just about $300 billion in tax revenues that did not have to be voted on by Congress. Had the inflation rate been just over 2.7 percent that year, the government would also have gotten the extra $30 billion in taxes, without all the drama.

---

1 What happened to the other $6 trillion? About $1 trillion or so is in the form of Treasury Inflation Protected Securities (TIPS). These debts have the special provision that if inflation reduces their real value, the federal government must make extra payments to the owners of the debts to compensate them. Thus, TIPS are protected from the inflation tax. The other $5 trillion is owned by the federal government itself, so what it collects in taxes from itself is exactly canceled out by the decline in the value of the dollar-denominated assets it holds.

SOME HISTORICAL EXAMPLES

From Rome in ancient times to Zimbabwe in the 2000s, governments around the world have succumbed to the temptation to use inflation to implicitly enhance their tax revenues. Sometimes the results have been catastrophic. After World War I, for example, Germany was required to provide **reparations** to the nations that had defeated it. Some of these reparations were in the form of gold or other physical assets.

Some reparations, however, were to be in the form of foreign currency—money issued by other nations. Germany did not have the foreign currency to make the payments, nor the conventional tax revenues to buy the foreign currency. So the German government simply started printing money to buy foreign currency to repay its debts. This caused inflation, which meant the government had to print even more money, which created more inflation, and so forth. Eventually, the price level in Germany was *doubling* every other day. The economy finally collapsed when people effectively refused to hold any German marks, forcing most voluntary trade within the country to a halt.

Although the German case is quite famous, there were more than 50 other hyperinflations during the twentieth century. In each case, the government involved printed money to pay for expenditures. The ensuing inflation effectively taxed those individuals and businesses that were either holding money or government debts denominated in money. Many of these hyperinflations came at the end of World War I or II, or after the Soviet Union broke up in 1991, although the Zimbabwean hyperinflation of the 2000s involved neither. In each instance, however, the source of the inflation was fundamentally the same: The government involved wanted to spend more than it could collect in other tax revenues. The revenue from the inflation tax made up the difference.

THE AMERICAN EXPERIENCE

Although the United States is unlikely to have a hyperinflation in the foreseeable future, our government has routinely shown a willingness to use inflation as a source of tax revenue. Most of the Revolutionary War was financed with an inflation tax, and both the Union and (especially) the Confederacy used the inflation tax to help finance the Civil War. In the twentieth century, all the significant wars in which the United States fought were financed in some part by the inflation tax, as were the more recent wars in Iraq and Afghanistan.

Although the mechanics for engineering the inflations have varied over time, the typical pattern since the founding of the Federal Reserve System (the Fed) in 1913 is simple. The U.S. Treasury issues bonds (borrows funds) equal to the difference between what Congress spends and conventional tax revenues. These bonds are then sold directly or indirectly to the Fed. The Fed pays for the bonds by creating deposits that the Treasury can use to pay its bills. As soon as the Treasury spends the funds, they become part of the money supply and begin putting upward pressure on the inflation rate. And as inflation rises, so too does the tax on people who hold currency (just about all of us), and the people who own federal government bonds whose values are fixed in dollar terms. Thus, although the Treasury is not physically "printing money," the consequences (on a smaller scale, of course) are just as they were when the German government printed money after World War I: more inflation and a higher inflation tax.

THE RECENT EXPERIENCE

Since January 20, 2009, the Treasury has issued an additional $6 trillion in bonds to finance its multi-trillion dollar spending splurge. This has produced rapid growth in the money supply, but not as much as would normally have been expected. Typically, the extra reserves created by the Fed to finance the Treasury spending would have been lent out by banks. Such lending creates new **demand deposits** and thus new money in circulation. But the Fed policy now pays interest on the reserves of **depository institutions** (such as banks). These interest payments give the institutions an incentive to hold onto more of the reserves created by the Fed, rather than lending the funds out to people and businesses. Thus, compared to what would have happened without the Fed interest payments, there has been less growth in the money supply, and so a lower inflation rate.

Nevertheless, the reserves are there in the banking system, ready to become new money, money that will fuel inflation. It would be possible for the Fed to "sterilize" these reserves by either (i) selling some of its enormous asset holdings to the banks, or (ii) asking the Treasury to pay off the debt held by the Fed. Neither seems likely. And because it also appears unlikely that the federal government will cut spending enough to match receipts from conventional taxes, this leaves only two possibilities: default or inflation.

THE LESSER OF TWO EVILS?

Technically, the federal government could eliminate some or all of our national debt by simply refusing to pay the debt when it is due: we could **default.** Over the centuries, this is a course that some nations have taken.

But this is not just embarrassing. It is also costly and inconvenient. After all, if a nation refuses to pay its debts, people will be reluctant to lend to it in the future. A politically more palatable solution is inflation. The Fed will simply fail to fully sterilize the reserves of the banking system. Hence, bank lending will grow more rapidly over time, causing the money supply to grow more rapidly, thereby ultimately causing a higher inflation rate. Money balances and federal bonds that are fixed in dollar terms will gradually shrink in **real value** and the burden of the national debt will gradually be reduced. There will be no ugly default. Instead the debt will be fully "repaid"—though, of course, it will be with dollars that are worth much less than those that were borrowed. And even though the inflation tax will add to the total tax burden, Congress will not have to go through the pain of voting this added tax into existence. The Fed will implement the higher taxes gradually and quietly over time, as it allows the inflation rate to rise. It is a solution that warms the heart of any good politician.

For Critical Analysis

1. If Congress manages to agree on higher income taxes, what do you predict will be true about the size of the inflation tax, compared to a scenario in which Congress fails to agree to raise income taxes?

2. Suppose a nation has $100 billion in currency outstanding, and $1 trillion in bonds, 30 percent of which are owned by agencies of the government. Assume that all the bonds are payable in the country's unit of account. Calculate how much revenue the government would collect in the form of an inflation tax if the inflation rate in the country was 2 percent. How much *extra* revenue from the inflation tax would be collected if the inflation rate was instead 5 percent? Show your calculations.

3. Analyze why many hyperinflations have been associated with wars or widespread civil unrest (or revolution). (*Hint*: Are wars expensive?)

4. The rule of 70 states that if something is growing at a rate of R percent per year, its value will double in 70/R years. Suppose the inflation rate becomes 5 percent per year in the United States. How long will it take for the price level to double? How long will it take for the real value of the current stock of federal debt to be cut in half? Show your calculations.

5. A hyperinflation is defined as one in which the inflation rate is at least 50 percent per month. Use the rule of 70 to calculate how many days it takes for the price level to double in a nation experiencing a minimum hyperinflation.

6. Average inflation rates tend to be higher in nations that have relatively weak judicial systems and property rights of the sort discussed in Chapter 1. Suggest some reasons why this pattern is observed.

CHAPTER 11

Is It Real, or
Is It Nominal?

Every few years, some important commodity, such as gasoline, electricity, or food, experiences a spike in prices. Reporters examine such price spikes and plaster newspapers, magazines, and Web sites with the appropriate headlines—sometimes relentlessly, day after day. TV commentators interview frustrated and worried Americans who spout the expected negative reactions to the higher prices of essential items in their budgets. The world, it would seem, is coming to an end.

Was Gas Really Expensive?

Let's just take one often-in-the-press example, gasoline prices. The authors of the book you are reading are old enough to remember the TV interviews that ensued when the price of gas first hit the unprecedented level of $1 per gallon, back in 1980. The same type of interviews occurred when the price of a gallon of gas broke the $2 barrier, early in 2005, and lodged above $3 in 2007. Not surprisingly, virtually the same interviews occurred when the price of a gallon of gas rose above $4 in the summer of 2008. At each point in time, everyone interviewed had the same response, even though years had passed between the different price spikes: "I guess I'll just have to stop driving." "I'm going to get a bike." "I'm selling my big car and getting a small one." And of course, each time there was an accompanying story about how record numbers of people were (or soon would be) flocking to their neighborhood motor scooter dealerships.

If we wish to sensibly analyze the effects of higher prices on the quantity demanded and the quantity supplied of any good or service in this world, we can rely neither on what journalists report nor on what

Americans say when they are interviewed. After all, what is important is not what people say but what they do. As economists, we best understand consumers by their **revealed preferences**. Similarly, business people are best understood by their actions, not their words. What people do is reflected in how much they actually buy of any good or service after its price changes, not by their complaints to a TV reporter or what they post on their blog or on Facebook.

RELATIVE PRICES, NOMINAL PRICES, AND INFLATION

For both microeconomic and macroeconomic analysis, the relevant price is the price *relative to* all other prices because people's decisions are based on **relative prices,** not **nominal prices.** The latter simply tell us the number of pieces of paper (dollar bills) you must hand over for a good. Nominal prices tell us nothing about the real sacrifice (measured in terms of other goods or of labor services) that one must make to obtain those goods. Relative prices reflect the real sacrifice involved in acquiring a good because they tell us the price of a good or service relative to the price of another good or service or to the average of all other prices. Relative prices tell us how much of other goods we must sacrifice.

Said another way, we have to separate out the rise in the general price level, called **inflation,** and the rise in the nominal price of a particular good or service. If *all* nominal prices went up exactly 3 percent, there would be no change in relative prices. This inflation of 3 percent would not change the real sacrifice entailed in acquiring any particular good. In the real world, even during periods of inflation, some prices go up faster than others and some prices even go down—witness the price of computing power, Blu-ray players, and smartphones. Nevertheless, if we want to predict people's behavior, we must know what has happened to the *relative* price of a good, and to determine this, we must adjust for inflation.

GAS PRICES REVISITED

Now let's get back to our example of gasoline prices. Your grandparents might be able to talk about buying gas for 30 cents a gallon (its average nominal price most of the time between 1956 and 1964). Today, what you pay in dollars per gallon is many times that level. People still drive nonetheless—indeed, the use of gasoline for cars and trucks in the United States is roughly triple what it was when the nominal price of gas was only 30 cents. Something must have happened. The most important "something" is a general rise in *all* prices, including gasoline prices.

In the summer of 2008, the price of gasoline spiked over $4 per gallon. One presidential candidate argued that the government should intervene on gas prices to "give families some relief." Two-thirds of American voters at that time said they thought that the price of gas was "an extremely important political issue." (Of course, when gas prices started tumbling in the fall of 2008, there were not many front-page articles or TV interviews with happy consumers, and the politicians simply became silent on this subject.) Consider, though, that at its nominal price at the beginning of 2009, the *relative* price of gas was back down to about what it had been in 1960—after correcting for overall inflation. For many people, this is a shocking revelation. But correcting for inflation is absolutely essential if you want to sensibly analyze the price of anything over time. Often we talk about the **real price** of a good or service. This refers specifically to subtracting the rate of inflation from the change in a nominal price over time. Not surprisingly, we also do the same exercise when we want to go from **nominal income** to **real income** over time.

THE IMPORTANCE OF HIGHER DISPOSABLE INCOME

Another fact is particularly relevant when thinking about the real burden of gasoline. People are becoming more productive over time because they are getting better educated and because ongoing technological change enables us to produce more with a given input of our time. As a result of this higher **productivity,** U.S. consumers' **disposable incomes** generally rise from one year to the next—and certainly rise on average over longer periods of time. As Americans become richer on average, they are financially able to handle even higher relative prices of those items they wish to purchase, gasoline included.

To help us understand this point better, researchers Indur Goklany and Jerry Taylor came up with an "affordability index." They compared family income to the price of gas from 1949 to 2008. They arbitrarily set 1960 at an affordability index of 1. Relative to this, a higher affordability index number means that something is more affordable. Even when gas was $4.15 per gallon, the affordability gas index was 1.35. In other words, the ratio of the average person's disposable income to the price of gasoline was higher by about 35 percent in 2008 than it was in 1960—gasoline was *more* affordable than it had been back in 1960, when your grandparents were filling up their tanks at 30 cents a gallon. That is hard to believe for some of us but true nonetheless. And once gas prices turned down at the end of 2008, the gas affordability index rose even more, passing 2, meaning that gasoline was more than twice as affordable at the beginning of 2009 as it had been in 1960. A subsequent rise in gas prices meant that by 2013 gas was "only" about 50 percent more affordable than it had been in 1960.

PRODUCT QUALITY CHANGES

The quality of gasoline typically does not change much over time. But the quality of many other products often changes significantly over time, usually for the better. Often we forget about this crucial aspect when we start comparing prices of a good or service over time. If you ask senior citizens today how much they paid for their first car, you might get prices in the range of $2,000–$5,000. The average new car today costs around $30,000 (in nominal dollars). By now, of course, you know that if you want to compare these numbers, you have to first account for the inflation that has occurred over whatever time period you are examining. In this instance, adjusting for inflation still means that the relative price of a car appears to be about 50 percent higher than it was, say, fifty years ago.

Does that necessarily mean that a car is really 50 percent more expensive than it was in 1960? Probably not. We must take into account improved quality features of cars today compared to those of the past. Today (unlike fifty years ago), the average car has the following:

- Antilock computer-controlled power brakes
- Power steering
- Digital radio with Bluetooth capability
- Air-conditioning
- Steel-belted radial tires
- Cruise control
- Power windows and locks
- Air bags
- Sixty percent better fuel economy

The list of improved and new features is actually much longer. Today, the average car is safer, breaks down less often, needs fewer tune-ups, has a host of amenities that were not even dreamed of fifty years ago, and almost certainly lasts for at least twice as many miles. If you correct not only for inflation but also for these quality increases, the relative price of cars today has almost certainly *fallen* appreciably in the past fifty years, in spite of the "sticker shock" that you may experience when you go shopping for a new car. That is, appearances to the contrary, the inflation-corrected **constant-quality price** of automobiles is actually lower today than it was five decades ago.

Declining Nominal Prices

The necessity of adjusting for inflation and quality changes continues to apply even when we examine goods whose nominal prices have declined over time. A good example is computing power. The nominal price of the average personal computer has gone down in spite of general inflation over the past several decades. These days, a Windows-based desktop computer has an average price of about $500. For a laptop, the average price is a bit over $600. A decade ago, the average machines in each category would have had nominal prices of twice as much. You might be tempted to conclude, then, that the price of personal computing has fallen by 50 percent. You would be wrong: The price has actually fallen by *more* than 50 percent.

Why? There are two reasons. First, over the past ten years, the average dollar prices of all goods increased by 30 percent. That is how much overall inflation there has been. That means that the *relative* price of the average computer has fallen by two-thirds, which, of course, is greater than 50 percent. But even here we are missing something extremely important: The quality of what you are buying—computing power—has skyrocketed. The processor speed of the average computer today is at least ten times greater than it was ten years ago and is increasing exponentially. Moreover, hard drives are bigger, tablets are more versatile, monitors are thinner, laptops are lighter, RAM is larger—the list of improvements goes on and on. And despite people's frustrations with both the hardware and software of the personal computer today, long-time users can tell you that both are vastly more reliable than they were a decade ago. Thus, if you only look at the inflation-corrected decrease in computer prices, you will be underestimating the *true* decrease in the relative price of computers.

The moral of our story is simple. At some point in your education, you learned that "what goes up must come down." Now you know that when it comes to prices, it is often the case that "what goes up has actually gone down." It is a lesson worth keeping in mind if you really want to understand the behavior of consumers and businesses alike.

For Critical Analysis

1. Create a list of goods (or services) whose quality has improved over time in such a way that the current prices of these commodities do not accurately reflect their real prices, even after adjusting for inflation. Now see if you can come up with a list of items whose quality has systematically *decreased* over time. Can you suggest why it is easier to find examples of the former than the latter?

2. The demand for small-engine motor scooters jumped when the price of gasoline started moving up in the summer of 2008. Make a prediction about the demand for this form of transportation in, say, two years from today. Explain your answer.

3. Explain why you will make more accurate predictions if you focus on the changing incentives people face rather than listening to what they say they are going to do.

4. When the price of gasoline rose to $4 from $2 per gallon, media commentators spoke as though people were headed to the poor house as a result. But here are some other facts: The average car is driven about 12,000 miles per year and gets about 24 miles per gallon. Even if people did not drive less when the price of rose, by how much did the average driver's "real" income fall due to the $2 per gallon rise in the price of gas? Given that per capita income is almost $50,000 per year, what is this income change in percentage terms? Show all calculations.

5. One implication of the **law of demand** is that the pain to a consumer of a price increase is always *less* than suggested by multiplying the price increase by the amount of the product consumed before the price increase. Explain why.

6. The law of demand also implies that the pleasure that comes from a fall in the price of a good is always *more* than implied by simply multiplying the price cut by the amount of the good consumed before the change. Explain why.

PART THREE

Fiscal Policy

CHAPTER 12

Who *Really*
Pays Taxes?

During (and even after) the election campaign of 2012, politicians had plenty to say about taxes. Some of the discussion focused on whether taxes should go up or down. But much of the talk was about who does— or does not—pay taxes. Some politicians (usually Democrats) claimed that high-income individuals ("the rich") do not pay their "fair share." Others (usually Republicans) claimed that the rich pay *more* than their "fair share." Regardless of party affiliation, most of the politicians had their own anecdotes to illustrate why their claims were correct. Let's see if some systematic data will illuminate this debate.

BURDENS AND FAIR SHARES

Economists have some well-defined and widely accepted ways to think about the "burden" of taxes (also called tax "incidence"). The simplest way to measure tax incidence (or burden) is to examine the share of taxes paid by different taxpayers. Thus, if $100 in taxes is collected and Alica pays $60, while Roberto pays $40, we say that Alicia bears 60 percent of the burden. This measure of tax burden (or incidence) is just the proportion of the tax bill paid by people. (All taxpayers are people in this discussion, because only people can pay taxes, whether they do so as workers, business owners, or whatever.)

Many commentators feel that this way of thinking about the burden of taxes is inadequate or misleading. Suppose, for example, that Alicia earns 80 percent of the income and Roberto earns the other 20 percent. One might argue that the relevant burden of taxes is *higher* for Roberto than for Alicia, because his share of taxes (40 percent) is so much higher than his share of income (20 percent). When looking across individuals or groups of individuals then, we might compare shares of total taxes paid with shares of total income earned.

A variant of this view is that it is useful to examine the share of each person's income that goes to paying taxes. Continuing with our example, suppose that Alicia's income is $240 and Roberto's is $60. Then 25 percent (= $60/$240) of Alicia's income goes to taxes, while approximately 67 percent (= $40/$60) of Roberto's income goes to taxes. This measure of the tax burden is called the **average tax rate.**

We cannot tell you which view of the tax burden is "better." What we *can* do is show you what these measures look like in the United States. Then you can decide on which you think is best—and you may then even decide you know whether or not various people are paying their "fair share."

In what follows, we shall be referring to all federal taxes, not just one portion or another of those taxes. We shall include federal income taxes, social insurance (Social Security and Medicare) taxes, corporate taxes, and even federal excise taxes (as are imposed on gasoline, alcohol, and cigarettes). We will also compare tax burdens across broad groups of people, so that we do not fall into the trap of thinking that the tax burden that happens to be borne by one or a few people is the relevant number to look at when deciding on national tax policy.

THE SHARE OF TAXES PAID

Let's look first at the simplest measure of the tax burden: What share of total federal taxes is paid by people at various income levels? First, we'll divide people up into "income quintiles." That is, we select the 20 percent of the people who earn the highest incomes and call this the top income quintile. Then we take the 20 percent of the population who earn the next highest incomes, and call this the second income quintile. We continue this process until we reach the 20 percent of the population that earns the lowest incomes, which we call the bottom income quintile. Then we ask the simple question: What share of total federal taxes is paid by each quintile? The answer is in column (1) of Table 12–1.

This comparison in column (1) is exactly like our initial comparison of the share of taxes paid by Alicia and Roberto. We see that the distribution of the tax burden is almost as striking as in our hypothetical example. The top quintile of income earners in the United States pays more than two-thirds of all federal taxes, even though only 20 percent of the population is in this group. When you hear people saying that "the rich" pay *more* than their fair share of federal taxes, this is the set of numbers that often are being referenced.

Although not shown explicitly in Table 12–1, the distribution of taxes paid is even more skewed toward the top income earners if we break the highest quintile into smaller units. For example, the people in the top 5 percent of the income distribution pay 39.6 percent of all federal taxes, while the rarified top 1 percent of earners pays 22.3 percent of all federal taxes. Another way to think about this is that the top 5 percent of earners pay more than the *combined* bottom four quintiles pay (31.8 percent), while the top 1 percent pays more than the combined bottom three quintiles pay (13.5 percent).

INCOMES VERSUS TAXES

Of course, the comparison in column (1) takes no account of the fact that people's incomes vary widely from top to bottom. Many people would argue that people with higher incomes have a greater ability to pay taxes, and thus they should be expected to pay more taxes. So, in column (2) we examine the share of total (before-tax) income that goes to each quintile. People in the top 20 percent of all income earners earn fully *half* of all income in the United States. Meanwhile, those in the bottom 20 percent earn only about 5 percent of all income. Equivalently, although people at the top pay much more in federal taxes than anyone else, the contrast between top and bottom is not nearly so dramatic if we take into account differences in income.

We come to similar conclusions if take a closer look among those people at the very top. Thus, the top 5 percent of income earners pull in 25.9 percent of all income in the United States, while the top 1 percent of earners collects 13.4 percent. Top earners fork over much more taxes than anyone else, but one key reason they do so is because they make much higher incomes.

Table 12–1 Incomes, Taxes, and Tax Rates (by income group)

Income Quintile	(1) Share of Federal Taxes (percent)	(2) Share of Income (percent)	(3) Average Tax Rate (percent)
Top quintile	67.9	50.8	24.7
Second quintile	18.3	21.1	17.5
Middle quintile	8.4	14.7	14.0
Fourth quintile	3.8	9.8	10.3
Bottom quintile	0.3	5.1	5.1

Source: Congressional Budget Office.

AVERAGE TAX RATES

Our final point of comparison of federal tax burdens comes in column (3) of Table 12–1. Here we see the average tax rate paid by people in different income quintiles. These numbers are calculated by adding up all federal taxes, adding up all incomes, and then dividing total federal taxes by total income. In the top quintile, people pay about $1 in taxes for each $4 of income, on average. In the middle quintile, people pay about $1 in tax for each $7 of income. At the bottom, taxpayers hand over $1 in taxes for each $20 in income.

These numbers seem to confirm our conclusions in the previous section regarding the burden of federal taxes. Although people at the top garner plenty of income, the taxes they pay rise even faster than their incomes do. Thus, the average tax rate rises rapidly as we move up the income ladder. Whether this is "fair" or not, we cannot say.

THE 91 PERCENT FANTASY

In 2012, some commentators argued that, since the decade of the 1950s, the burden of taxes on the rich had actually *fallen*. The centerpiece of this claim was based on the **marginal tax rate** over time. The marginal tax rate is simply the proportion of an *additional* dollar of income that goes to taxes. Thus if a person pays $100 in taxes on the first $1,000 in income and $200 in taxes on the second $1,000 in income, we say that the marginal tax rate on the first $1,000 is 10 percent, while the marginal tax rate on the second $1,000 is 20 percent. (Note a person making $2,000 would pay a total of $300 in taxes, and so pay an *average* tax rate of 15 percent.)

It is true that in 2012 the marginal federal tax rate for top income earners was about 38 percent, depending on exactly the form in which their income is earned. It is also true that in, say, 1958 the marginal tax rate at the top was 91 percent. But there was a key difference between the two years: Large numbers of high income earners in 2012 were actually *paying* the top marginal tax rate. Almost *no one* was paying the top marginal tax rate back in 1958, even the richest of the rich. In fact, so few people paid it that the Internal Revenue Service (IRS) will not reveal the exact number, because that number is so small you might be able to figure out who was paying it—which would violate IRS rules on taxpayer confidentiality. (We do know that 236 out of 45.6 million taxpayers were paying rates of 81 percent or higher, so the 91 percent tax rate must have applied to an even smaller number of people.)

Five decades ago, people at the top earned much more than the average amount of income and paid much more than the average amount in federal taxes. To illustrate, in 1958 the average tax rate on people in the top 5 percent of the income distribution was almost double the average tax rate in the middle of the distribution—just as it is today. Thus, although the marginal tax rate at the top may have come down dramatically, the average tax rate has not. Whether this is fair or not, we cannot say.

FACTS VERSUS . . .

Elections tend to bring out the best and the worst in humans. The rhetoric can be magnificent, but the disregard for facts (and worse, the venture into fantasy) can be just as striking. Over the century or so that income taxes have been levied in the United States, two facts have been true. First, incomes have been distributed unequally. Second, taxes have been distributed even more unequally, with people's tax bills rising even faster than their incomes as they move up the income distribution. Reasonable people can disagree over whether or not—in their opinion—the rich should pay more (or less) than they do in fact pay. But for there to be any hope that these disagreements will lead to sensible public policy, the rhetoric should at least be based on facts rather than fantasy or falsehood.

FOR CRITICAL ANALYSIS

1. Suppose that on the first $10,000 of income people must pay 10 percent of their income in taxes. Also suppose that for the next $10,000 in income they must pay 20 percent in taxes, and for the next $10,000 they must pay 30 percent in taxes. Compute the average and marginal tax rates for each of three people who earn (respectively) $5,000, $15,000, or $25,000.

2. Referring back to the previous question, suppose that each of these people is paid the same before-tax hourly wage, but that they work 500 hours per year, 1,500 hours per year, and 2,500 hours per year, respectively. Calculate the after-tax hourly wage that each is earning. Comparing these people, who would you say likes leisure the most (compared to work)? Who likes leisure least compared to work?

3. When comparing the share of income going to various quintiles in this chapter, we used before-tax income. Suppose, instead, we had used after-tax income. Given what you learned about the taxes people pay, would the difference in shares of "income" between top and bottom be larger or smaller? Explain, briefly.

4. If you were a politician who wanted to make the case that the rich are taxed "too heavily," which column in Table 12–1 would you feature in your speeches?

5. In 2012 President Obama said that when it comes to taxes "for some time now, when compared to the middle class, [the rich] haven't been asked to do their fair share." For this question, assume that people in the middle income quintile are the middle class and that the people in the highest income quintile are the "rich." Based on what you learned in this chapter, would you agree with the president? Does your answer change if the "rich" are those people in the top 5 percent or top 1 percent? (*Hint*: Be sure to do what the president did not do: Define what you mean by "fair share.")

6. Although just about everyone who works pays Social Security and Medicare taxes, roughly 47 percent of such people pay either *zero* federal income taxes or *negative* federal income taxes. What do you suppose the attitude of these people is when a politician proposes an increase in federal income tax rates? Would their attitude likely be different if the politician proposed raising Social Security and Medicare tax rates?

CHAPTER 13

Are You Stimulated Yet?

George Bush supported one. Barack Obama proposed one too. And Republicans and Democrats in both houses of Congress ended up passing two of them. With all of this backing, surely economic stimulus packages must be good for the economy, right? Well, maybe not. Let's see why.

STIMULUS PACKAGES

As implemented by the U.S. (or foreign) governments, so-called economic stimulus packages generally contain some combination of two elements: higher government spending and lower government taxes. One consequence of such packages is that the size of the government **deficit** grows, implying that the **national debt** must get larger. Higher debt is merely a side effect of a stimulus package, however. The *objective* of such packages is to increase total spending in the economy, raise employment, and reduce the unemployment rate.

Proposals for stimulus packages generally come during economic recessions, when **gross domestic product (GDP)** is depressed and the unemployment rate is elevated. At first blush, it seems like a government stimulus is exactly what we need at such times. After all, government spending is part of GDP, so more government spending seemingly must, as a matter of definition, generate more GDP. And because the things that the government buys (such as cement for new highways) are produced using labor, it seems pretty clear that more people will be hired, thereby cutting the unemployment rate. Alternatively, to the extent that part of the stimulus comes in the form of a tax cut, this puts more **disposable income** in the hands of consumers, some or all of which will presumably be spent by them. Again, production of goods and services rises and the unemployment rate falls. Either way, it seems, a government stimulus package is the sure-fire way out of a recession. Before we jump to this conclusion, however, it will be wise to take a closer look.

TAX CUTS

Let's look first at the tax cuts that are often components of stimulus packages. To do so, imagine for the moment that we keep government spending at current levels and simply cut the taxes we are collecting from people during the current period. Such an action is what people have in mind when they refer to a "tax cut." To fully appreciate the effects of a tax cut, however, we must carefully specify how it is conducted. For example, in the "Economic Stimulus Act of 2008" the tax cut consisted of **lump sum tax rebates.** Each eligible person received $300, regardless of income, with another $300 for each dependent child.[1] In contrast, tax cuts pushed by President Kennedy in the 1960s, President Reagan in the 1980s, or President Bush in the early 2000s reduced the **marginal tax rate** for many taxpayers. That is, the taxes taken out of additional dollars of earned income were reduced. This not only lowered the individual's **tax liability** (total taxes owed), it also increased the incentive to work more, produce more, and thus earn more, because taxpayers could keep more of what they earned.

However the tax cut is implemented, it is clear that if the government is going to pay for its spending, at least initially it must borrow, that is, run a budget deficit. Unless potential lenders are convinced they will be repaid, they will not lend, and the only way for the government to repay its loans is to collect *more* taxes in the future. Indeed, future taxes must rise by enough to repay both the principal and the interest on the loan.

Now we see the problem with trying to stimulate the economy by cutting taxes: A reduction in *current* taxes must be met by an even larger increase in *future* taxes. For a given level of government spending, taxes *cannot* actually be reduced. They can at best only be moved around in time. Thus, although a "tax cut" puts more current disposable spending in the hands of consumers, it also loads them up with an even bigger added debt burden. In the case of tax cuts of the rebate variety, this is the end of the story. The added debt burden will weigh on the spending decisions of consumers, so there is no particular reason to think

---

1 For individuals earning over $75,000 or couples earning over $150,000, the rebate was gradually phased out to zero and thus technically not lump sum. This actually tended to discourage some work effort among these individuals, which would tend to reduce real GDP. This effect was likely quite small, however, because the dollar amounts were small.

that consumers will spend more today. They may just save most of the increase in disposable income so they'll be ready in the future when their bigger tax bills come due. Of course, consumers may not *think* this way about their taxes at all. But the key point is how they *behave*. And the fact is that many consumers act *as though* they are quite conscious of the added burden of future taxes they bear when current taxes are cut.

Stanford researchers led by John B. Taylor have examined the impact on consumer spending of both the Economic Stimulus Act of 2008 and the American Recovery and Reinvestment Act of 2009. The researchers found that neither the tax rebates of 2008 nor the cash transfers and tax rebates of 2009 had any measurable impact on consumer spending, despite all the predictions by the politicians. In the words of Taylor and his colleagues: "The stimulus didn't work."

Reductions in marginal tax rates offer hope of something more. Again, we cannot expect people to go on a spending spree just because taxes have been moved around in time. But there is an added feature with lower marginal tax rates. People have an incentive to work more, produce more, and thus earn more, because they get to keep a larger share of what they earn. This feature of this type of tax cut does indeed stimulate the economy, although it does so from the supply side (labor supply rises) rather than the demand side. Indeed, many researchers attribute much of the prosperity of the 1960s and the 1980s to the cuts in marginal tax rates implemented by President Kennedy and President Reagan in those decades.

Spending Increases

Now, what about the other half of stimulus packages—higher spending by the government? To sort this out, we will first have to distinguish between two broad types of government spending: that which is a substitute for private spending and that which is not. For example, although the government spends plenty on education (primary, secondary, and college), so do private citizens. The government spending is a substitute for private spending, and when the government spends more on education, private spending on education falls. This offsetting change in private spending clearly reduces the potential stimulus effect of the government. Indeed, in some cases, education included, it appears that *all* of the higher government spending is offset by lower private spending. The stimulus effect in this instance is obviously zero.

Of course, plenty of government programs do not compete directly with private spending. For example, most defense spending (such as expenditure on the war in Afghanistan) does not compete with private spending. Also, some so-called infrastructure spending, such as on highways and bridges, competes little with private spending. Thus, when government defense or infrastructure spending goes up, there is no direct dollar-for-dollar cut in private spending, as there can be with items like education. Nevertheless, there are generally substantial *indirect* impacts on private spending—impacts that can markedly reduce the stimulating effects of the government spending. Let's see why.

INDIRECT OFFSETS IN PRIVATE SPENDING

As we suggested above, the real burden of the government is its spending. Taxes are simply the means of deciding who shall bear that burden. Thus, for a given level of other expenditures, when defense or infrastructure spending rises, taxes *must* rise, at some point now or in the future. And because consumers know this, they will typically make some provision for it, by reducing their own spending. This clearly dampens the overall stimulus effect of the higher government spending.

There is another potential offset when government spending rises. If the government "finances" this spending by borrowing rather than raising current taxes, the result can be upward pressure on interest rates. Higher interest rates in turn reduce the attractiveness of consumer durable goods (such as houses and cars) and also reduce the profitability of business investment spending. Thus, when larger government deficits push up interest rates, private consumption and investment spending will decline, once more dampening any hoped-for stimulus.

DELAYS IN SPENDING

As amazing as this may seem, there is yet one more obstacle in the path of stimulus spending—time. Despite all the headlines about so-called "shovel ready" projects and "immediate action," there are usually long delays in implementing the spending portion of stimulus packages. Let's consider one simple example. As part of the 2009 stimulus pushed by President Obama and passed by Congress early in that year, more than a dozen states were supposed to get federal funds for building or expanding light rail commuter systems. Ultimately, two of the states (Wisconsin and Ohio) decided that the benefits of this spending to them would not outweigh the costs. Hence, these states declined to accept the money for light rail systems, hoping the federal government would let them keep the money and use it to repair and expand their roads and bridges. In fact, late in 2010 (nearly two years after the stimulus package was passed) President Obama ordered that the rejected funds be redirected to the dozen states that had accepted the rail funding. Well into 2011 most of these funds were still unspent, as were many billions of dollars of other funds included in the "2009" stimulus package.

Not all spending is delayed this much, of course (although some can be delayed even more). But the key point is simple. Despite all of the claims politicians make about taking "immediate action," it just does not work out this way. In fact, over the span of the last fifty years or so, much of the government spending supposedly designed to help pull us out of recessions was not actually spent until well after these recessions were over.

THE STIMULUS THAT MOSTLY WAS NOT

The 2009 American Recovery and Reinvestment Act (ARRA), President Obama's first major piece of legislation, received lots of media attention, in no small part because of its size—$862 billion. But its impact on aggregate demand appears to have been minimal. One reason stems from the fact that a large portion of the legislation called for grants to state and local governments. The law's backers argued that these funds would immediately be spent by the recipients on all sorts of new programs, thereby stimulating the economy. In fact, the state and local governments used almost *all* of these transfers to reduce their borrowing. Thus, the mechanics went like this: The federal government borrowed funds (about $120 billion per year during each of the first two years), lent those funds to the states, which then borrowed $120 billion less. Net effect: Federal debt went up, state and local debt down, and aggregate spending remained unchanged.

The ARRA was also touted as being big on infrastructure—roads, bridges, and so forth. In fact, the legislation itself never called for more than about 10 percent of its funds to be used in this way, and by two years after its passage, only a small fraction of this had been spent. Indeed, by 2010, government purchases of goods and services had risen only $24 billion, and infrastructure had gone up only $3 billion. In a $14 trillion economy, these sums were trivial. It is perhaps little surprise then, that Robert Barro of Harvard found that the ARRA had only a tiny stimulus effect during the recession itself. Barro also estimates that once the need for subsequent tax hikes is factored in, the overall impact of President Obama's "stimulus" bill will be a *reduction* in GDP.

IS STIMULUS POSSIBLE?

As you may have gathered, our overall conclusion is that unless marginal tax rates are reduced, we should typically not expect government stimulus packages to actually stimulate the economy very much. Lump sum tax cuts are not really tax cuts at all, and higher government spending levels are routinely offset in whole or in part by cuts in private spending. But notice our use of the word "typically." There is indeed a set of circumstances in which stimulus packages have the potential to live up to their billing. Fortunately, these circumstances do not come around very often. Indeed, the only time they are likely to have been observed is during and immediately after the Great Depression (1929–1933).

A series of declines in aggregate demand over the period 1929–1933 ended up pushing economy-wide output down by 30 percent and raising the unemployment rate to an unprecedented 25 percent of the labor force. By the depths of 1933, many people had been unemployed for years, and they and their families were living hand to mouth. They were **cash-constrained.** Every time their income changed by a dollar, so too did their spending. Thus, when so-called "relief" spending by the federal government began, most people worried not a bit about the future tax liabilities that might be involved. Moreover, much of the spending was on items (such as the Hoover Dam, and Post Office and other public buildings) that did not compete directly with private spending.

This set of circumstances meant that the government stimulus spending during the 1930s did help increase total spending and also helped get people back to work. Indeed, it was during this period that stimulus spending first gained credibility among both economists and politicians. But the circumstances of the 1930s were extreme. No recession since then has come remotely close to being as severe, not even the recessions of 1981–1982 and 2007–2009. Moreover, since the 1930s credit markets have become much more developed. People have credit cards and lines of credit and thus the ability to continue spending even when their incomes decline. To be sure, a prolonged period of unemployment can eventually exhaust these reserves. Fortunately, the number of people who find themselves in such circumstances is generally small, even in recessions. As a result, the stimulating effects observed for stimulus packages during the 1930s cannot be expected to be repeated, unless of course the 1930s somehow repeat themselves.

So our moral is that if you have not felt stimulated by federal spending increases or tax cuts, do not feel left out. You have plenty of company.

FOR CRITICAL ANALYSIS

1. Why is it in the interest of politicians to promote the notion that unemployment can be lowered if federal spending is increased?

2. If the unemployment rate can be reduced by cutting taxes, why don't we cut taxes to zero, at least during recessions?

3. During World War II, federal spending rose to roughly 50 percent of total spending in the economy, from its prewar level of just under 10 percent. How was this possible—that is, what spending had to decline to make it feasible for the federal share of spending to rise by a factor of five?

4. Some people argue that unemployment benefits (i.e., cash payments by the government to people who are unemployed) help stimulate the economy. The reasoning is that without the benefits the incomes of unemployed people would be lower, and thus their spending on goods and services would be lower. Keeping in mind that unemployment benefits are generally no more than 40–50 percent as large as the typical earnings of people when working, answer these questions:

   i. How do unemployment benefits change the incentive to be *employed*? Explain.

   ii. Is it possible that a system of unemployment benefits could actually cause total spending in the economy to *fall*? Explain.

5. If current taxes are reduced by way of a lump sum rebate, does the consumer response likely depend on how long it will be before taxes are actually raised to pay off the debt incurred by the government? In answering, be sure to account for the fact that the longer the delay in raising taxes, the greater will be the interest debt that accrues.

6. Who is more likely to think of a cut in current taxes as being a true reduction in taxes: a young worker with several young children or an older retiree with no children? Explain.

CHAPTER 14

The Fannie Mae, Freddie Mac Flimflam

Between 1995 and 2012, the U.S. housing market went on the wildest ride in its history. Over the years 1995–2005, median real (inflation-adjusted) house prices soared 60 percent nationwide and then promptly crashed, falling 40 percent from 2006 to 2012. Over the same period, the proportion of Americans who owned homes, normally a variable that changes quite slowly, leapt from 64 percent to 69 percent and then quickly dropped back to 65 percent. Meanwhile, the number of new houses built each year soared from 1.4 million to 2 million and then plunged to 500,000 per year.

But what really got people's attention—and created huge pressures on financial markets here and abroad—was the fact that just as quickly as people had snapped up houses during the boom years of 1995–2005, they simply *abandoned* their houses beginning in 2006, refusing to make any more payments on their mortgages. In a typical year, about 0.3 percent of homeowners (fewer than one out of three hundred) stop making mortgage payments and thus have their houses go into foreclosure, a process in which the borrower must give up any **equity** (ownership) in a home because of a failure to meet payment obligations. The foreclosure rate doubled to 0.6 percent in 2006, doubled again in 2007, and rose yet again in 2008, 2009, and 2010, before leveling out. In some hard-hit states, such as Nevada, foreclosures exploded to more than *ten times* the normal nationwide rate, with one home out of thirty going into foreclosure each year.

Across the country, people were literally walking away from their homes, leaving them in the hands of banks and other lenders. These lenders then took huge financial losses when forced to sell the abandoned properties in a market in which house prices were already falling. The result was further downward pressure on prices, which gave more owners the incentive to walk away from their homes, which raised foreclosures, and so forth. Within just a few years, the housing market was more depressed than it had been at any time since the Great Depression of the 1930s. In fact, to see what happened, we need to go back and start our story during that very period.

SOME HOUSING HISTORY

Before World War II, most home mortgages were of short duration, such as one or two years (rather than fifteen to thirty years, which is common now). During the Great Depression, many risk-weary lenders refused to renew mortgages when they came due. The state of the economy was such that most borrowers were unable to repay immediately, and so their homes were foreclosed. In response, the U.S. government in 1934 created the Federal Housing Administration (FHA), to guarantee some home mortgages from default, and in 1938 created the Federal National Mortgage Association (FNMA, known as Fannie Mae), to purchase mortgages from the FHA, enabling the latter to guarantee still more mortgages. In 1968, Congress authorized Fannie Mae to buy mortgages from virtually all lenders, and it also created Ginnie Mae (the Government National Mortgage Association), authorized to bundle up, guarantee, and sell home mortgages issued by the FHA. Two years later, in 1970, Congress created Freddie Mac (the Federal Home Mortgage Loan Corporation) to offer competition to Fannie Mae. Both Fannie Mae and Freddie Mac are referred to as **government-sponsored enterprises (GSEs).** They are technically independent of the federal government, but both are subject to congressional oversight and, it turns out, to political pressure to do what Congress wants them to do. Ginnie Mae is part of the U.S. Department of Housing and Urban Development and thus under the direct budgetary control of Congress.

It has been clear from the inception of each of these agencies that the intent of Congress has been to promote home ownership in the United States, especially among lower-income individuals. Ultimately, the only way to do this is to reduce costs for borrowers. The agencies have done this in a variety of ways, including allowing people to make down payments of as little as 3.5 percent of the value of the house, as opposed to the 10–20 percent required by private lenders.

Going back as far as 1993, Fannie and Freddie have taken special measures to subsidize the highest-risk borrowers, along the way racking up huge potential risks. But beginning soon after the recession of 2001, Congress made it clear to Fannie, Freddie, Ginnie, and the FHA that even more should be done. In fact, powerful Democratic Representative Barney Frank explicitly told the agencies that they needed to "roll the dice" in the housing market, that is, take on more risk by insuring, guaranteeing, or making home mortgage loans to people who were much worse credit risks than normal. The organizations responded with enthusiasm, helping to spark the housing boom that finally ended up crashing. Two things made the outcome of this behavior singularly costly. First, at the behest of Congress, the agencies focused most of their efforts on subsidizing purchases by the least creditworthy customers. Second, when it became apparent just how extensive the foreclosure losses were going to be, Congress not only bailed out the agencies by giving them more taxpayer cash but also told them to continue doing more of the same. The result will be huge tax bills for you.

ROLLING THE DICE

The two riskiest types of mortgages are called subprime and Alt-A, respectively. Subprime mortgages are those made to borrowers who are considered to have a much higher than normal risk of defaulting. These people have relatively poor credit scores, and the size of the mortgage they are getting is high relative to their ability to repay. Alt-A mortgages are generally those that either are missing some key documentation (such as proof of the borrower's income) or have especially low down payments. Either way, Alt-A mortgages are riskier than the typical mortgage, and most are considered part of the subprime market.

By 2008, Fannie Mae and Freddie Mac either owned or were guaranteeing nearly 10 million subprime and Alt-A mortgages. The outstanding balance on these loans was $1.6 *trillion*, a potential liability of $8,000 for each U.S. taxpayer. What made this worse, however, is that since the early 1990s Fannie and Freddie had routinely misrepresented just how risky their portfolios were becoming, reporting that their subprime and Alt-A mortgages were "prime" mortgages (the highest-quality, least risky category).

BAILOUTS

As we saw, both Fannie and Freddie were established as GSEs, that is, privately owned, but publicly sponsored, or endorsed. Although the federal government did not formally guarantee either organization, many people regarded such a guarantee as being implicit. Indeed, when it became apparent in September 2008 that both organizations were **insolvent** (their liabilities exceeded their assets), that implicit guarantee became reality. The federal government initially offered up $200 billion in explicit guarantees. Since then, the size of the guarantee—many people refer to it as a bailout—has been increased twice. In fact the federal government essentially took over temporary control of Fannie and Freddie, and the Obama administration announced that there was *no limit* on how much the federal government was willing to invest in the two institutions. As of the end of 2012, actual losses suffered by taxpayers had mounted to $137 billion, although many more billions—perhaps trillions—of dollars could be at risk if the economy turns down again.

At this point, you might think that Fannie and Freddie would change their behavior, perhaps by turning to lower-risk loans, or even trying to clean up their balance sheets by getting rid of the worst loans. In fact, both agencies have done just the reverse, getting involved in even riskier loans and helping borrowers avoid their debts at little or no cost to the borrowers. The result is that the likely cost to taxpayers continues to rise.

Cash Unlimited

As a practical matter, Fannie Mae and Freddie Mac have gotten themselves involved in almost every nook and cranny of the U.S. housing market. Consider just two examples. First, plenty of people in the housing market are either "underwater" (the value of their home is less than what is owed on it) or simply unable or unwilling to continue making payments on the mortgage. Fannie and Freddie have been actively engaged in a loan forgiveness program for many of these people, although this is not what the program is called. Essentially, the two agencies have been purchasing existing mortgages that are in default and then "modifying" them by reducing the amount the borrower owes. Rather than reporting this as a debt forgiveness (something that likely would not sit well with homeowners who are still paying their bills), Fannie and Freddie just report the forgiveness as a "credit-related expense."

Of course, some people just cannot or will not continue making payments, even when offered a substantial reduction in the amount of the mortgage. In these cases, Fannie and Freddie have been taking over ownership of the homes—at a rate of one every ninety seconds. By 2010 the two agencies owned 170,000 homes, more houses than are located in Seattle. After putting still more cash into the properties (about $10,000 per house) to ready them for sale, the agencies then hand them over to real estate agents to sell for whatever price they can get—which of course is always far below what was owed on them. And the borrowers? Well, they are off the hook, replaced by the taxpayers.

It May Get Worse

The meltdown in housing markets slowed the issuance of new mortgages by banks and thus slowed the growth of Fannie and Freddie. While this may help reduce future losses by these two organizations, it will not stem the overall flood of losses. Why not? It is simple. The FHA has dramatically *increased* the amount of lending it is undertaking, and as a practical matter virtually all FHA loans are made to borrowers who are riskier than average. Moreover, the risks of FHA loans are enhanced by the fact that it requires a down payment of only 3.5 percent of the value of the home. Some experts now believe that up to one in ten of all FHA loans will end up in default—which means that taxpayers will be footing the bill.

Just how costly the federal involvement in mortgage markets will become is anyone's guess. In the meantime, the federal government seems determined to keep the cash flowing, which means that your tax bill will keep on growing. How high it will go, no one knows.

For Critical Analysis

1. Who benefits from the actions of Fannie and Freddie?

2. There are approximately 220 million taxpayers in the United States, at least as measured by the number of tax returns filed with the IRS. But only about half of these "taxpayers" end up paying income taxes. (Some of the others pay only Social Security or Medicare taxes, while some actually *receive* payments, under the Earned Income Tax Credit program.) Considering that Fannie and Freddie are now owners or guarantors of almost $5.5 trillion in mortgages, what is the maximum potential liability for each of the taxpayers who actually pay income taxes?

3. How does the FHA requirement of a low down payment affect the incentive of the borrower to default on his or her mortgage, that is, stop making the payments? What impact does this have on taxpayer liability for these loans? Explain.

4. What characteristics of the people in a congressional district would help explain whether the member of Congress representing that district favored or opposed the actions of Fannie Mae and Freddie Mac? Explain.

5. Why do low-income and high-risk borrowers receive subsidies from Fannie, Freddie, Ginnie, and FHA? Make sure you address the question of why the government does not simply hand them cash every year, rather than subsidizing their purchases of houses.

6. Given the huge losses incurred by Fannie and Freddie as a result of "rolling the dice," why do you suppose Congressman Barney Frank was not voted out of office?

CHAPTER 15

Big Bucks
for Bailouts

Alstom, American International Group (AIG), Anglo Irish Bank, Bear Stearns, Citigroup, General Motors (GM), Chrysler, Freddie Mac, and Fannie Mae. What do these companies—which are based in a variety of nations and offer different products—all have in common? They have been "saved" by government (read: taxpayer) subsidies. They were, according to proponents of these subsidies, just "too big to fail." Now that concept—too big to fail—could be looked at in the alternative. Perhaps those companies were too big to save—at least from the points of view of taxpayers and the long-run efficiency of each country's economy. We shall first look at what "too big to fail" means and then examine this concept in the context of what has been called **industrial policy.**

THE LOGIC (OR ILLOGIC) BEHIND
TOO-BIG-TO-FAIL POLICIES

The people who support preventing very large corporations from failure, whether those companies are manufacturers of high-speed trains, insurance providers, investment banks, commercial banks, automobile producers, or large guarantors of mortgages, sincerely believe that a failure of a very large corporation can create **systemic risk,** that is, threaten a widespread reduction in economic activity throughout an economy.

Consider two contrasting examples. Your local CD retailer is having a tough time competing against online downloads. Eventually, the company goes out of business, laying off its three employees and abandoning the rented retail space in the local mall. There are no systemic risks with such an event. A few people have to look for jobs and the landlord of the rented space has to find another tenant, but that is the extent of the impact of the firm's closure.

Now consider GM. For years before its partial takeover by the government, it was losing hundreds of millions, even billions, of dollars per year. Over the last half century or so, during good economic times GM routinely agreed to generous labor contracts. During bad economic times, it was stuck with high labor costs, including high pension benefits (see Chapter 16). By the time the recession of 2007–2009 rolled around, GM was simply uncompetitive due to its high costs. Just as the company was about to go under, it was saved by the U.S. government (with subsequent help from the Canadian government). Those who argued for government intervention claimed that GM's bankruptcy would put several hundreds of thousands of people out of work and lead to a vicious cycle of increasing unemployment throughout the United States and elsewhere. In other words, GM was too big to fail and had to be saved. The systemic risks were supposedly too great to let it go under.

THE MORAL HAZARD PROBLEM

When large corporations are "saved" by the government, the taxpayers who actually pay the bill also face the possibility of a **moral hazard** problem. Why? Consider how labor leadership and management in corporations can reason if they believe they are candidates to be "saved." Believing that they will not be allowed to fail, they can engage in activities that are not necessarily in the long-term interests of the company. (And, we should add, not in the interests of the taxpayers—that's you and us—who will be subsidizing them.)

When times are tough, the head of a labor union whose workers produce GM's cars knows that the union does not have to "give back" very much to the company in terms of lowered fringe benefits and lower wages. Why should it? The company is too big to fail, after all. The managers of GM act the same way: They know that during tough times they do not have to institute dramatic cost-saving actions because—you guessed it—GM is too big to fail.

This moral hazard problem influenced the behavior of all of the large corporations that were saved by taxpayers in the United States—Chrysler, Citicorp, Goldman Sachs, and AIG, among others. Those companies' workers and managers were no longer subjected to an unfettered competitive marketplace, and they acted accordingly. The result was (and continues to be) the **inefficient** use of resources. Costs were not trimmed where and when they should have been, excessive risks were assumed, and so forth. As a result, resources were not employed in their most productive uses. So, not only are taxpayers footing the bill, but also the economy will in general grow less rapidly than it would have without the subsidies to the too-big-to-fail corporations. The citizens of the United States are poorer as a result.

THE BIG WINNERS IN DETROIT

Now, you might think that fat-cat stockholders were the chief beneficiaries of bailouts. Sometimes they are—but not always. Consider the bailout of GM and Chrysler in 2009. When these companies nominally went bankrupt, much of the companies' indebtedness was to the pension and health insurance plans of the United Autoworkers (UAW). Under normal bankruptcy law, the unions would have to get in line along with all of the other creditors. But President Obama moved the UAW to the front of line. Researchers James Sherk and Todd Zywicki have shown that because of this special priority, other creditors and U.S. taxpayers lost plenty, but the members of the UAW were virtually untouched by the bankruptcy. In fact, taxpayer losses on GM and Chrysler bailouts matched almost dollar for dollar the gains that accrued to the pensions and health plans of UAW members. Union members working for GM did not even have to take a pay cut. Shareholders and other creditors, meanwhile, took big losses.

INDUSTRIAL POLICY IS BACK IN FASHION

The latest worldwide recession officially lasted from 2007 to 2009, but its reverberations may still be going on as you read this. The recession brought back in vogue something called **industrial policy.** The too-big-to-fail policies examined above are just an example of this policy. The way President Barack Obama put it in 2009 was this: The government must make "strategic decisions about strategic industries." The $800 billion stimulus legislation in that year earmarked billions of taxpayer dollars for investment in "strategic" sectors, such as renewable energy, advanced vehicles, and high-speed rail systems. But the United States was not alone. At about the same time, Japan announced that it would create a strategy to make sure that its key industries would not be "left behind." France declared that it would invest in "strategic" industries, too, although the government there used the phrase "national champions." The bottom line is that an essential part of the new industrial policy in Europe and Asia, as in the United States, has been to lavish taxpayer subsidies on banks, carmakers, and other favored industries.

If we define industrial policy as attempts by governments to promote the growth of particular industrial sectors and companies, history does not shed a favorable light on these policies. Simply claiming, as Obama did when he visited Detroit in 2010, that taxpayer subsidies "saved jobs" does not really tell us anything. After all, the correct analysis of any industrial policy must compare costs with benefits. How much did those "saved" jobs cost the economy?

Consider the example of the semiconductor industry. Japan spent somewhere between $20 and $50 billion (estimates differ) during the early 1980s to make the Japanese firms in this industry competitive. All that money was spent for naught. None of the Japanese firms appreciably improved their market shares, and the two world leaders in the industry today are American (Intel) and South Korean (Samsung). Singapore spent about $15 billion in 1995 as part of a similar drive, as did China in 1999. Both policies were failures—no companies from either nation have managed to crack the top ten.

Britain tried similar maneuvers, just as it tried to prop up some of its ailing car companies. Both efforts failed. France spent billions trying to construct an information technology industry, a move that ultimately failed also. The simple fact is that the more globally competitive an industry is, the harder it is for government industrial policy to effectively promote companies in that industry. And because virtually all major industries are globally competitive, this means that industrial policy is destined to fail.

Picking Winners—Not as Easy as It Seems

Most industrial policy is based on the belief of government officials that they are able to pick winners. Whether the selection process is undertaken in a poor country or in a rich country does not seem to matter, for reasons that are easy to understand. Consider the incentives facing government employees in charge of industrial policy compared to the incentives of decision makers in the private sector. First, the government policymaker is using other people's money—taxpayer dollars, yen, or euros. It is difficult for us to imagine that a government employee using other people's money is going to make better predictions about which industries or companies are going to be winners in the future than someone who has "skin in the game." After all, if the government employee is wrong, the financial consequences are minimal. Her or his life savings are not at stake.

There is also a certain amount of arrogance involved in a government official deciding where best to move resources in the economy.

Under what circumstances would such an official have better information about future demands for certain products or services than people in the private sector? There are almost none of which we can think.[1] After all, those who pick winners in the private sector are rewarded handsomely and can become millionaires or even billionaires. In contrast, a government official who is successful in this endeavor might move up a grade level in civil service rating or perhaps be mentioned as an exemplary employee. Small peanuts, we would say.

CREATIVE DESTRUCTION AND BANKRUPTCY

Do you know what a Polaroid camera is? Probably not, because that good has essentially disappeared due to competition from a better instant photography medium—digital cameras. Do you know what an eight-track cassette tape is? Probably not. It was replaced by the compact disc, which is now becoming obsolete because of competition from online music downloading. Have you ever heard of FedMart? Probably not. It was eventually put out of business by innovative competitors, such as WalMart.

A Harvard economist named Joseph Schumpeter (1883–1950) had a term for the death of certain companies over time—**creative destruction.** He used this term to describe the process by which the economy is transformed by innovation. In his view (now generally shared by economists), innovative entry by entrepreneurs is the economic force behind sustained long-term **economic growth.** In the process of innovation, the value of established companies (and many of their specialized workers) is destroyed. Of course, at the same time, even *more* value is created elsewhere by the innovation. Indeed, the process of creative destruction is at the heart of sustained economic growth.

We see most dramatically the process of creative destruction at work when we see companies going **bankrupt.** Many companies simply disappear when they go bankrupt, forcing employees to seek work elsewhere. Other companies emerge from bankruptcy leaner and better able to compete. When a bankrupt company emerges from bankruptcy, most of its creditors and shareholders have lost considerable sums. Many of its workers have been laid off or have had to accept reduced salaries and benefits, even if they previously had a union contract. That is what would have happened, without taxpayer subsidies, for GM, Chrysler, Citicorp, Goldman Sachs, and AIG.

---

1 The (possible) exceptions involve industries (such as aerospace) where correct decision making is heavily dependent on "top secret," government-held information.

BUT WHAT ABOUT SAVING JOBS?

Whether bankruptcy is involved or not, creative destruction necessarily means that people will have to move from one job to another—old jobs are eliminated, new ones created. Supporters of the too-big-to-fail theory (and of industrial policy in general) always argue that they are only trying to "save jobs." It is true that such taxpayer subsidies may protect the jobs of those in the subsidized companies or industries. But that is hardly job-saving **fiscal policy.** Every subsidy to save a job in a company or industry has to be paid for. Either there is less government spending (and presumably fewer jobs) elsewhere or taxes must be raised, which means less taxpayer spending (and presumably fewer jobs) elsewhere. Therefore, a job "saved" in one company or industry ultimately leads to job *losses* in unsubsidized companies and industries. (In fact, there is every reason to believe that the jobs lost will *exceed* the jobs saved—see Chapter 27.) Economists are fond of saying that there is no such thing as a free lunch, and this principle applies to any fiscal policy justified as being purportedly "job saving."

NEGATIVE INDUSTRIAL POLICY

Despite all the talk by politicians about "saving" jobs, governments at all levels in the United States regularly have acted in ways that *reduce* employment. Indeed, the tax and regulatory policies of the federal government and many state governments have fostered a climate of **deindustrialization.** The United States has the second highest corporate tax rate in the world. Perhaps equally important, federal government regulations add dramatically to the cost of production in the United States. Estimates of the annual costs go as high as $1.7 trillion for federal regulations, or about 12 percent of annual national income.

Businesses in the United States today are also facing regulatory uncertainty. They do not know whether there is going to be a tax on carbon output. They certainly do not know how to estimate the costs of the 2,400-page health care law, or the 2,300-page financial services law, both passed in 2010. The latter requires that 243 new rules be written and by 2013 only a few had been finalized. The health care law ("Obamacare") involves over a hundred new agencies, all of which will write new rules. Only a few of these rules had trickled out by 2013. All of this uncertainty puts U.S. companies at a disadvantage to their competitors in other countries, particularly in Asia.

The bottom line is simple. Despite their willingness to spend your money on bailouts, politicians do not actually seem too interested in promoting the policies that would encourage long-run recruiting and retention of workers. Once again, good politics makes bad economic policy.

For Critical Analysis

1. Who benefits and who loses from our "too-big-to-fail" policies?

2. Why do you think politicians are more active creating industrial policies during recessions than during boom times?

3. Estimated U.S. taxpayer subsidies in green energy technology through 2013 are about $125 billion. Under what circumstances does the federal government need to undertake these subsidies as opposed to letting private companies themselves pay for such investments?

4. Outline the scenario of what would have happened to GM had the federal government allowed it to go bankrupt on its own several years ago?

5. What is the incentive that private companies have to "pick winners"?

6. Is there any way to stop creative destruction?

CHAPTER 16

The Pension Crisis

It is never too early to think of your future. We refer not to your future classes or what you will do when you graduate. Nor do we speak of your future family, should you choose to have one. And not your self-imposed plan to stay healthy in the future. Rather, you might want to start thinking about how big your pension will be when you retire. That may seem a long way off, but for some—those who go to work for some cities and for some states—your pension might start in just twenty years.

CALIFORNIA IS NOT CALLED THE "GOLDEN" STATE FOR NOTHING

Today, in the face of one of its most serious fiscal crises ever, California taxpayers are footing the bill for former police officers, firefighters, and prison guards who can retire at age 50 with a pension that equals 90 percent of their final year's salary. There are more than 15,000 government retirees in California who receive pensions that exceed $100,000 per year (and this does not count payments from federal taxpayers through the Social Security system).

Consider the odd case of Gary Clift. He spent twenty-six years in the California Department of Corrections & Rehabilitation. Then he retired. He now collects 78 percent of the $112,000 salary he earned in his last year of work. He also gets full health care coverage for life, which adds a tidy sum to his retirement package. Ironically, Clift spent his last two years at work analyzing legislation that would raise the state's expenditures on retirement benefits. He got nowhere when he raised a red flag about increasing pension costs. As he said, "It's just taxpayers' money, so nobody cares."

Before we go any further with the relationship between government pension payments and California's fiscal problems, let's first look at the concept of retirement and pensions.

To Retire, Normally You Have to Save

If we look back in time far enough, the concept of retirement did not exist. Individuals worked until they were physically unable to continue and died soon thereafter. That was back when just about everyone in the world was poor. Those who could not work were often cared for by family members in large households. Not surprisingly, in very poor countries today, having lots of kids continues to be a form of retirement security—in fact, they may be the only thing standing between a retiree and starvation.

Through **economic growth,** individuals in many nations have been able to **save** to create **wealth** that can be used later on. If you do not **consume** everything that you earn, you can put aside funds to purchase houses and to make investments. Hence, when you choose to give up gainful employment, you have a stock of wealth that you can draw down during your remaining years.

If you work for a large company or a government, your retirement benefits will likely come from a pension plan run by your employer. Hopefully (for you), your employer will put aside funds in investments that will yield enough income to provide you with your promised pension. If the actual **rates of return** on these investments turn out to be as predicted by the pension plan, there will be enough funding for all employees who retire to receive their promised pensions. If this condition is satisfied, we say that the employer (company or government) has a **fully funded pension liability.** Whenever employers do not set aside enough funds to cover future pensions, we say that they have **unfunded pension liabilities.** Now let's go back to the state of California to see how it has become the king of unfunded liabilities.

The Golden State Turns Red

The term "red ink" usually refers to losses being suffered by a private company or to current year **budget deficits** incurred by a government entity. California's red ink of this variety has lately been in the neighborhood of $20 billion per year. But recent California budget deficits are peanuts compared to its unfunded liabilities, mainly due to contractually guaranteed future pensions for its employees.

In the last dozen years, California state revenues—mainly from taxes—increased about 25 percent. Pension costs for that state's public employees, in contrast, increased by about 2,000 percent. No, that is not a typo. Recall our example of Gary Clift above. When he retired from the Department of Corrections & Rehabilitation, he was eligible to apply for a disability "bonus" that would have added many thousands of dollars to his pension every year. Gary had this option not because he was disabled, but because the state of California says that working for the Department of Corrections is stressful—and so an employee *might* become disabled. Gary did not put in for the disability bonus, but he was the only manager at the prison where he worked that did not.

California's problem is more widespread than simply the prisons, however. In the 1960s, about 5 percent of retiring California state workers received so-called public safety pensions. That meant the individuals had been working in a "dangerous" job. Today, about 35 percent of retiring state workers obtain this "public safety" retirement bonus, which was intended originally just for firefighters and police officers. In addition, California is the only state that uses the last year of an employee's salary to determine her or his long-term pension benefits, rather than averaging over the salaries of the last several years of work. Because pay usually rises over time, California's method generates extra pension benefits—and extra liabilities for taxpayers.

But there is more. Every year for decades, the legislature in Sacramento has improved public pension benefits. Consider just one of those improvements, passed in 1999. It was supposed to cost the state about $650 million per year by 2010. It actually cost $3.1 billion in 2010 and $3.5 billion in 2011.

Okay, so how bad can it be—a few billion here and a few billion there? Well, California has admitted to a $288 billion unfunded pension liability, but some independent estimates imply the liability may be much higher. Moreover, this problem cannot go away by itself because the courts have consistently upheld government employee pension benefits as untouchable contracts, except in a few rare cases in which a local government declares bankruptcy. In one recent year alone, over $3 billion of California state spending was diverted to pension costs from other programs. The diversion of state spending to fund pensions seems certain to do nothing but rise in the future. Even the state's 2012 decision to enact $55 billion in pension "reforms" will hardly make dent in the problem.

A Closer Look at the "Garden State"

New Jersey, the self-described "garden state," is starting to look wilted. It, too, has been running billions of dollars of pension red ink per year. By the latest estimates, the New Jersey employee pension fund is $36 billion in the hole. That may sound small compared to California, but consider what it means for a typical four-member household in New Jersey. Each such family is on the hook for about $16,500 in tax liabilities, just to make up this underfunding.

How did New Jersey get in this mess? Well, as in California, a big part of the problem started back in the 1990s. The stock market was booming, producing high rates of return on state investments. Under the assumption that these abnormally high returns were the new reality, state legislatures enhanced retirement benefits. Two stock market crashes later, the hoped-for returns have not materialized, but the promised pensions are still there.

THE TOTAL PICTURE

Throughout the United States, only four states—Florida, New York, Washington, and Wisconsin—have well-funded pension systems. The remaining states are facing different degrees of fiscal disaster. Illinois and Kansas, for example, have enough assets on hand to pay for only 50–60 percent of their pension liabilities.

The PEW Center on the States did an exhaustive study just before the 2008 financial meltdown and concluded that the fifty states had a $1 *trillion* pension funding gap. The states combined had contractually promised $3.35 trillion in pension, health, and other retirement benefits but only had $2.35 trillion on hand to pay for them. Despite some reforms in state plans since then, this $1 trillion gap is still there. Most states continue to make unrealistic assumptions about future rates of return despite the low actual rates they have earned since 2008. (And, by the way, cities are also in deep trouble. One conservative estimate puts the funding gap for them at nearly $600 billion.)

THE PRIVATE SECTOR HAS PROBLEMS, TOO

Do not think that government decision makers at the state and local level have been the only ones to create unfunded pension liabilities. In the private sector, large corporations have found themselves with growing pension funding problems. One major company that has long loved to hide future pension liabilities is General Motors (GM). In an effort to report better earnings, that company routinely used aggressive accounting practices and made pension contributions that were just a fraction of what it really needed to make. Eventually, though, GM's actual pension promises became due. When the company tried to pay for these costs by hiking the price of the cars it manufactured, those cars quickly became uncompetitive. Consumers started buying other brands that were cheaper for the same quality. The result was GM bankruptcy and a federal takeover. Taxpayers ended up with a large percentage of shares in "Government Motors," as it came to be called. This put taxpayers on the hook for future pension liabilities of the company.

GM is not alone. Over 75 percent of the largest five hundred corporations in the United States have unfunded pension fund obligations. It is perhaps no surprise that many of these companies have lobbied Congress to let them off the hook from meeting their legal obligations to more fully fund their pension plans.

BANKRUPTCIES ON THE HORIZON?

Returning our examination to the public sector, even though you may not be expecting to retire for decades, your economic well-being is already changing because of retirement commitments that cities and states have already made. To fulfill those unfunded pension liabilities, city and state governments are cutting back on essential services—education, police and prisons, and firefighters. You might think that we should not or "cannot" let essential government services be cut back just to pay pension benefits. Right now that is reality, however, all across the country.

Is there a way to reduce unfunded pension liabilities? Yes, but it is ugly. Just ask the residents of Vallejo, California. In 2008, eighteen police personnel and firefighters unexpectedly retired early. That city of 120,000 was immediately obligated to pay out several million dollars for their first year of retirement. This is a city that was already forking over $220 million for pensions and health care. Vallejo City government filed for **bankruptcy.** Stockton, California (population 300,000) followed Vallejo with a bankruptcy in 2012, driven importantly by the city's $800 million in unfunded pension and health plan liabilities.

Under so-called Chapter 9 of our **Bankruptcy Code,** municipal governments can propose their own reorganization plans and void union contracts without having to sell off their assets, such as buildings and investments. The public pension obligations of Vallejo were lumped together with all the rest of its obligations. Everyone from private accounting firms to public pensioners who were owed money had to take a "haircut"—accept less than 100 cents on the dollar owed. So now we see at least one way that cities, indeed, even states, can get out of the jam in which they find themselves. Declaring bankruptcy can allow them to renegotiate future pension benefits to put them more in line with future funding possibilities. Stockton has now followed the same path.

Right now, some cities are defaulting on the loans that they took out in past years. In a recent year, $3 billion in city debt was not paid when it came due. As we have already seen, that is a trivial amount compared to total unfunded pension liabilities. When more municipal governments choose to go bankrupt, the rate of municipal bond defaults will increase accordingly. This process will be painful and costly for retirees and bondholders alike. But the simple fact is this: State and local governments have been making promises they cannot realistically keep. Something must give and that means one of three things must happen. State and local spending on other programs must be slashed, taxes have to be hiked dramatically, or pensions need to be cut. Eventually, the easy political promises of the past must collide with the hard economic reality of the future.

WHY IS THE FEDERAL GOVERNMENT NOT IN THE SAME FIX?

As you might have noticed, there has been little discussion of the federal government's retirement system to which all of us contribute—**Social Security.** The reason is that Social Security is a **pay-as-you-go system.** The federal government has *not* taken your Social Security "contributions" and invested them in some special account. Indeed, there is no "account" earning interest now so that it will be there with your name on it when you choose to retire in your sixties. While you may have heard about something called a Social Security trust fund, that fund is just on paper. It is a myth, and a huge liability itself, about which you will learn more in Chapter 18.

FOR CRITICAL ANALYSIS

1. If there is no government- or company-provided pension system, how can an individual create a financially safe retirement?

2. Why would a state or local government ever commit more resources for future pension benefits than it could possibly have resources to pay?

3. Many state and local governments have been using an assumed 8 percent rate of return figure when calculating future funding of promised pension benefits. Why do you suppose they used this rather than an assumption of 2 percent, or even 0 percent?

4. Why can state and local governments not simply continue to borrow funds through the bond market to cover not only shortfalls in current

tax revenues but also shortfalls in future available funding to pay contractual pension benefits?

5. The weak economic climate since 2008 has caused many workers to defer their retirements. How will this affect large employers in state and local governments?

6. In the private sector, one in five workers have been promised lifetime pensions. In the public sector, four in five workers have lifetime pensions. Why does the private sector offer so few lifetime pensions compared to the public sector?

CHAPTER 17

Higher Taxes Are in Your Future

"These road improvements of $241,000,000 were paid for:

86 percent from the Federal Highway Trust Fund
12 percent from state funds
2 percent from local funds."

Most of you have seen at least one sign similar to this while driving somewhere in the United States. If you have ever driven anywhere in Europe, you see comparable signs, but they usually have a longer list of "contributors." The parallel, though, is that the "contributors" are government agencies, not *you*. Now, it would be nice to think that funds for highway improvement projects come from the moon or Mars or even from the bank account of some foreign oil mogul. But they do not.

THOSE PESKY BUDGET CONSTRAINTS

Government does not exist independently of those who live, work, spend, and pay taxes in our society. As an economy, we face a **budget constraint.** Whatever is spent by government—federal, state, or local— is not and cannot be spent by individuals in the nation. Whatever government commands in terms of spending decisions, private individuals do not command. All of those dollars available for spending on final goods and services in the United States can be controlled by you, the private citizen, or government. Otherwise stated, what the government spends, you do not spend. It is as simple as that, despite the periodic efforts of government (especially at the national level) to conceal the truth of this budget constraint.

Stimulus and Bailout

Early in 2008, as the recession of 2007–2009 worsened, President Bush proposed, and Congress enacted, an "economic stimulus" package said to cost $152 billion. Most of the package consisted of tax cuts that were supposed to raise disposable income and thus produce an increase in private spending. As we noted in Chapter 13, however, neither these tax cuts, nor similar provisions in President Obama's 2009 "stimulus" package, had *any* measureable impact on consumption spending.

Later in the year, as the recession continued to worsen and financial panic hit, the president and Congress reacted by bailing out some of the biggest financial companies in the United States, including insurance giant AIG. The legislation implementing these bailouts called for up to $700 billion in taxpayer funds to be used to prop up the companies.

Just a few months later, newly elected President Obama successfully pushed Congress in 2009 to pass yet another stimulus package, this one said by the Congressional Budget Office to cost $833 billion. This legislation provided additional money for extended unemployment benefits and also transferred hundreds of billions of dollars to state and local governments.

Not long afterward (ironically, just as the recession was officially ending) President Obama pushed for and got funds to bail out the major American automobile companies. Ford declined the funds, but both General Motors (GM) and Chrysler accepted the money, enough in the case of GM to make taxpayers of the United States majority shareholders in the company.

Taken together, the stimulus and bailout programs enacted over this eighteen-month period had a price tag of somewhere between $1.5 and $2 trillion. Remarkably, even though these programs were supposed to be temporary, federal spending continued at unprecedented levels through 2012. All in all, during his first term in office, President Obama managed to spend $6 trillion *more* than the federal government collected in tax revenues. For four years in a row, we thus had federal budget deficits that were larger than any experienced ever before in American history. Because all of these new debts will have to be repaid, higher taxes are in your future.

Increased Spending, Increased Taxes

When Congress passes legislation to spend more, whether it is for bailing out the financial sector, improving education and public infrastructure, or attempting to reduce poverty, there is ultimately only one place it can obtain the resources. That place is you and everyone else who earns income each year in the United States. As we noted in Chapters 13 and 14, having the ability to run a larger federal government deficit (and thus increase the net national debt) does not change the fundamental budget constraint facing our society.

What government spends, the rest of us do not spend. Perhaps without your realizing it, your **real tax rate** has already gone up in the last several years. Why? Because federal government spending has increased as a share of **gross domestic product (GDP).** Your real tax rate is easily calculated. It is the percentage of GDP controlled by the government. Since 2000, that number has risen from 18 percent of GDP to 24 percent of GDP. You may not have felt the bite yet, but the observed taxes that you pay through automatic withholding of federal income taxes on your wages or salary will eventually catch up. The budget constraint guarantees that.

But What about All Those Tax Cuts?

By the time the election of 2010 rolled around, taxpayers were finally starting to get nervous about all of this new federal spending. But the economy was still going sideways coming out of the recession of 2007–2009, so the first thing Congress did after the election was to extend tax cuts passed back in 2001 and 2003, during the Bush Administration. Moreover, Congress extended unemployment benefits (even though the recession had ended eighteen months before) and even enacted a temporary cut in the payroll taxes used to finance Social Security. (The cut was supposed to last two months. It actually lasted two years.)

As we noted above and in Chapter 13, such "tax cuts" cannot be expected to increase aggregate demand—and in fact they did not. Because government spending was not reduced, the burden of the government was not reduced. The net effect was to raise the deficit relative to what it would have been and make the necessary eventual tax increases even larger. No matter what the politicians promise, the budget constraint cannot be avoided. Hence, higher taxes are in your future.

There was one tiny bright spot. Because **marginal tax rates** were reduced as part of the 2010 package, people likely worked more, produced more, and thus earned more in 2011 and 2012, because they get to keep more of what they earned. This "supply side" effect of the lower tax rates probably helped the economy recover a bit faster from the recession of 2007–2009.

The flip side came in 2013, when Congress voted to return the payroll tax to its previous, higher, level. Congress also hiked federal income taxes on individuals making more than $400,000 per year. Taken together, these measures will likely generate about $60 billion a year in tax revenues. They will also reduce the incentive to work, and so dampen the level of real economic activity.

WHO GETS THE BILL?

Although almost 220 million personal tax returns are filed with the Internal Revenue Service every year, many of these filers pay no federal income taxes at all. In fact, about 47 percent of "taxpayers" either pay no federal income taxes or actually pay *negative* federal income taxes because they receive **tax credits.** Under a tax credit, people who pay no federal income taxes effectively get a check from the federal government, which they can use to pay other federal taxes they might owe (such as Social Security) or to pay *future* federal tax liabilities, should they arise. If there *are* no current or likely future tax liabilities, well, they get to keep the cash.

There may well be perfectly good reasons to effectively exempt some people from paying income taxes, perhaps because they are impoverished or have major medical bills. But it is important to recognize two implications of shielding large numbers of people from income taxes. First, this helps create the impression for many voters that federal spending is effectively "free"—because, after all, they will not be responsible when the bills come due. Thus, they are more likely to favor expansion of government spending that does not confer benefits that exceed its costs. This reduces the overall wealth of society. Second, with large numbers of individuals exempt from federal income taxes, the burden on those who *do* pay taxes is that much greater. This will induce such people to work less, produce less, and earn less because they get to keep less of what they earn. This lower production means that the wealth of society is reduced.

IS ARGENTINA SHOWING THE WAY?

Argentina was one of the ten richest countries in the world a hundred years ago. It has since slipped to about 70th on that list. Over the same period, government spending in Argentina has been growing relative to the overall size of the economy, as have taxes there. Not too long ago, Argentine president Cristina Kirchner announced that the nation's private pension system was being taken over by the national government. While she claimed that it was for the "good of the people" because the market was too risky for retirement savings, in fact President Kirchner wanted to use those assets to fund more government spending. Technically, the government will "borrow" from the retirement system. But because the Argentine government has a track record of defaulting on its borrowings, many people expect that they will get back few, if any, of their hard-earned retirement pesos.

As you might expect, contributions into the private pension plan plummeted as soon as the government announced its plan. Some Argentine citizens quietly began moving other **assets** out of the country, hoping to protect them from similar confiscation. Still others began making plans for moving *themselves* out of the country, on the grounds that emigration was the ultimate form of protection.

The Argentine government's nationalization of the private pension system is simply a once- and-for-all increase in taxes. While it is unlikely that the U.S. government would seek to take control of private pension plans here, the Argentine story illustrates the key point of this chapter. What the government spends, we must pay for. Sometimes the government must be creative in making that happen, but happen it will. Hence our prediction: Higher taxes are in your future.

FOR CRITICAL ANALYSIS

1. The government now owns shares of stock and warrants in many companies that were bailed out. (Warrants are rights to own future shares of stock.) If the value of the shares owned by the federal government increases because the market price per share rises, in what way could this increase actually permit a reduction in future taxes? Explain.

2. If you are a lower-income-earning individual and thus pay no income taxes, should you care about tax increases for other individuals? Explain.

3. Is it *possible* that in, say, ten years, the real tax rate paid by U.S. residents will be lower than it is today? What circumstances would have to change to make this occur? Explain.

4. Who, exactly, will be paying the higher future taxes implied by the stimulus packages, tax cuts, and bailouts of 2008–2012? (*Hint:* Look in the mirror.)

5. Why do most politicians love to spend money and hate to pay for their expenditures? Is this attitude different from the one you have toward making purchases as opposed to paying for those purchases? What are the consequences for you if you spend more than your income?

6. Most states have laws or constitutional provisions that require them to quickly eliminate any budget deficits by either raising taxes or cutting spending. Can you suggest why states would have this rule, but the federal government would not?

CHAPTER 18

The Myths of Social Security

You have probably heard politicians debate the need to reform Social Security. If you are under the age of 30, this debate has been going on for your entire lifetime. Why has nothing been done? The reason is that the politicians are debating over "facts" that are not facts: Most of the claims made about Social Security are myths—urban legends, if you like. Sadly, the politicians have been repeating these myths so often for so long that they believe them, and so do their constituents (perhaps including you). As long as these myths persist, nothing meaningful will be done about Social Security, and the problem will simply get worse. So let's see if we can cut through the fog by examining some of the worst Social Security myths.

MYTH 1: THE ELDERLY ARE POOR

The Social Security Act was passed in 1935 as the United States was emerging from the Great Depression. The **unemployment rate** at the time was the highest in our nation's history. **Bank runs** and the stock market crash of 1929 had wiped out the savings of millions of people. Many elderly people had few or no **resources** to draw on in retirement, and their extended families often had few resources with which to help them. In the midst of these conditions, Social Security was established to make sure that the elderly had access to some *minimum* level of income when they retired. It was never meant to be the sole source of retirement funds for senior citizens.

Given the circumstances of the program's founding, it is not surprising that many people associate Social Security with poverty among the elderly. The fact is that both the Social Security program and the financial condition of older people have changed dramatically over the years. For example, measured in inflation-adjusted dollars, initial Social Security payments were as little as $120 per month and reached a maximum of $500 per month, or about $6,000 per year. Today, however, many recipients are eligible for payments in excess of $30,000 per year. More important, people over age 65 are no longer among the poorest in our society.

Despite the ravages of the recession of 2007–2009, today's elderly have accumulated literally *trillions* of dollars in **assets.** These assets include homes and substantial portfolios of stocks and **bonds.** In addition, millions of older Americans are drawing *private* pensions, built up over years of employment. Social Security payments, for example, now provide only about 40 percent of the income of the average retired person, with the rest coming about equally from private pensions, employment earnings, and investment income. Far from being the age group with the highest poverty rate, the elderly actually suffer about 25 percent *less* poverty than the average of all U.S. residents. To be sure, Social Security helps make this possible, but just as surely, only about 9 percent of the elderly are living in poverty. In contrast, the poverty rate among children exceeds 20 percent.

Myth 2: Social Security Is Fixed Income

Most economic and political commentators and laypersons alike treat Social Security benefits as a source of fixed income for the elderly, one that supposedly falls in **real purchasing power** as the general **price level** rises. This myth, too, has its roots in the early days of Social Security, when payments were indeed fixed in dollar terms and thus were potentially subject to the ravages of **inflation.** But this is no longer true. In 1972, Congress decided to link Social Security payments to a measure of the overall price level in the economy. The avowed reason for this change was to protect Social Security payments from any decline in real value during inflation. In fact, because of the price level measure chosen by Congress, the real value of payments has actually each year there is inflation (which is almost every year).

Although there are many potential measures of the average price of goods and services, Congress decided to tie Social Security payments to the **consumer price index (CPI).** The CPI is supposed to measure changes in the dollar cost of consuming a bundle of goods and services that is representative for the typical consumer. Thus, a 10 percent rise in the CPI is supposed to mean that the **cost of living** has gone up by 10 percent. Accordingly, the law provides that Social Security benefits are automatically increased by 10 percent.

As it turns out, however, the CPI actually overstates the true inflation rate: It is *biased upward* as a measure of inflation. This bias has several sources. For example, when the price of a good rises relative to other prices, people usually consume less of it, enabling them to avoid some of the added cost of the good. But the CPI does not take this into account. Similarly, although the average quality of goods and services generally rises over time, the CPI does not adequately account for this fact. Overall, it has been estimated that until recently, the upward bias in the CPI amounted to about 1.1 percentage points per year on average. Revisions to the CPI have reduced this bias to about 0.8 percentage points per year. Thus currently, if the CPI says prices have gone up, say, 1.8 percent, they have really gone up only 1.0 percent. Nevertheless, Social Security payments are automatically increased by the full 1.8 percent.

Now, 0.8 or 1.1 percentage points do not sound like much, and if it happened only once or twice, there wouldn't be much of a problem. But almost every year for forty years, this extra amount has been added to benefits. Over a long period, even the small upward bias begins to amount to a real change in **purchasing power.** Indeed, this provision of the Social Security system has had the cumulative effect of raising real (inflation-adjusted) Social Security benefits by about 50 percent since the early 1970s. Therefore, despite the myth that Social Security is fixed income, in reality the benefits grow even faster than inflation. By the time you read this, Congress may have switched Social Security indexation to a price index that does a better job of measuring the true inflation rate, but plenty of damage has already been done.

MYTH 3: THERE IS A SOCIAL SECURITY TRUST FUND

For the first few years of Social Security's existence, taxes were collected, but no benefits were paid. The funds collected were used to purchase U.S. Treasury bonds, and that accumulation of bonds was called the Social Security Trust Fund. Until 2010, tax collections (called **payroll taxes**) exceeded benefits paid each year—so that the trust fund grew to about $2.5 trillion in Treasury bonds. Benefits now exceed tax revenues because retiring baby boomers are collecting more and paying less. The bonds will have to be sold to finance the difference. By around 2035, all of them will be sold, and thereafter all benefits in excess of payroll taxes will have to be financed explicitly out of current taxes—or benefits will have to be cut by about 25 percent.

The standard story told (by politicians at least) is that the bonds in the trust fund represent net assets, much like the assets owned by private pension plans. *This is false.* Congress has already spent the past excess of taxes over benefits and has simply given the trust fund I.O.Us. These I.O.Us are called U.S. Treasury bonds, and they are nothing more than promises by the U.S. Treasury to collect taxes from someone to pay benefits. When it is time for the trust fund to redeem the I.O.Us it holds, Congress will have to raise taxes, cut spending on other programs, or borrow more to raise the funds. But this would be true even if there were *no* Treasury bonds in the trust fund: All Social Security benefits must ultimately be paid for out of taxes. Thus, whatever might have been intended for the trust fund, the only asset actually backing that fund is nothing more and nothing less than an obligation of Americans—you— to pay taxes in the future.

Myth 4: Social Security Will Be There for You

Social Security was a great deal for Ida Mae Fuller, who in 1940 became the first person to receive a regular Social Security pension. She had paid a total of $25 in Social Security taxes before she retired. By the time she died in 1975 at the age of 100, she had received benefits totaling $23,000. And although Ida Mae did better than most recipients, the *average* annual real rate of return for those early retirees was an astounding 135 percent *per year*. (That is, after adjusting for inflation, every initial $100 in taxes paid yielded $135 *per year* during each and every year of that person's retirement.)

People retiring more recently have not done quite so well, but everyone who retired by about 1970 has received a far better return from Social Security than could likely have been obtained from any other investment. These higher benefits relative to contributions were made possible because at each point in time, *current retirees are paid benefits out of the taxes paid by current workers*. Social Security is a **pay-as-you-go system.** It is not like a true retirement plan in which participants pay into a fund and receive benefits according to what they have paid in and how much that fund has cumulatively earned. Thus, as long as Social Security was pulling in enough new people each year, the system could offer benefits that were high relative to taxes paid. But the number of people paying Social Security taxes is no longer growing so fast, and the number of retirees is growing faster. Moreover, today's trickle of new retirees is becoming tomorrow's flood as the baby boom generation exits the workforce. The result is bad news all around.

One way to think about the problem facing us—which is chiefly a problem facing *you*—is to contemplate the number of retirees each worker must support. In 1945, forty-two workers shared the burden of each Social Security recipient. By 1960, nine workers had to pick up the tab for each person collecting Social Security. Today, the burden of a retiree is spread out among slightly more than four workers. By 2030 or so, fewer than three workers will be available to pay the Social Security benefits due each recipient.

The coming tax bill for all of this will be staggering. If we *immediately* raised Social Security (payroll) taxes from 15.3 percent to a bit over 19 percent—more than a 24 percent increase—and kept them there for the next seventy-five years or so, the system's revenues would probably be large enough to meet its obligations. But this would be the largest tax increase in U.S. history, which makes it extremely unlikely that it will occur. Yet every day that Congress delays, the situation gets worse. If Congress waits until 2030 to raise taxes, they will have to be increased by more than 50 percent. Indeed, some commentators are predicting that without fundamental reforms to the system, payroll taxes *alone* will have to be hiked to 25 percent of wages—in addition to regular federal, state, and local income taxes, of course.

What are any reforms likely to be? Well, rules will specify that people must be older before they become eligible for Social Security benefits. Existing legislation has already scheduled a hike in the age for full benefits up to 67 from its current 66. Almost certainly, this age threshold will be raised again, perhaps to seventy. Moreover, it is likely that all Social Security benefits (rather than just a portion) will eventually be subject to federal income taxes. It is even possible that some high-income individuals—you, perhaps—will be declared ineligible for benefits because their income from other sources is too high.

So, what does all this mean for you? Well, technically, a Social Security system will probably be in existence when you retire, although the retirement age will be higher than it is today and benefits will have been scaled back significantly. Strictly speaking, the Social Security Trust Fund may even still be around when you hit the minimum age for benefits. But whatever else happens to the Social Security system between now and your retirement, you can be secure in your knowledge of one thing: You will be getting a much bigger tax bill from the federal government to pay for it.

FOR CRITICAL ANALYSIS

1. Where has all of the Social Security money gone?

2. People over the age of 65 have been highly successful in protecting and enhancing the real benefits they receive from Social Security. This has come at the expense of other people in society, particularly

young people. What do you think explains the ability of older people to win political battles with younger people?

3. Analyze how each of the following hypothetical policy changes would affect people's decision to retire. Would the change induce people to retire sooner or later? Explain your reasoning.

   a. An increase in the age at which one can receive full Social Security benefits (currently age 66 to 67, depending on the year in which a person was born)

   b. A decrease in the fraction (currently 75 percent) of full benefits that one can receive if retirement occurs at age 62

   c. An increase in the Medicare eligibility age from its current level of 65

   d. An increase to 100 percent from its current 85 percent in the maximum fraction of Social Security benefits that is subject to the federal income tax

4. If a person starts collecting Social Security benefits before full retirement age but also continues to work, then for each $2 in income earned (above a modest level), that person's benefits are reduced by $1. What is the effective **marginal tax rate** imposed by the Social Security system on such earnings from work? Explain.

5. For each year after full retirement age that a person delays collecting Social Security benefits, the annual benefits are raised by 8 percent. (This "bump" in benefits ceases at age 70. Additional retirement delays do not cause benefits to rise any further.) How is the incentive to retire before age 70 affected by this provision for benefit increments, relative to a system in which benefits were not raised in this manner? Explain.

6. What does the existence of the Social Security system do to the incentive of a worker to save for his or her retirement? What does it do to the worker's incentive to save to provide an inheritance for his or her children? Explain.

PART FOUR

Monetary Policy and Financial Institutions

The Fed and Financial Panics

The Panic of 1907 began after a failed attempt by Otto Heinze to "corner the market" on **shares of stock** in the United Copper Company. Heinze had expected the demand for United's shares to increase in the near term and thought that if he bought up enough shares quickly at low prices, he could turn around and sell them at a handsome **profit.** His judgment proved wrong, and Heinze had to sell out at devastatingly low prices. Not only did his stock brokerage firm go out of business as a result. More disastrously, the public's confidence in the financial condition of banks that had large holdings of United Copper shares evaporated. Confidence also plummeted regarding the financial health of several banks with whom Otto's brother Augustus was associated.

All of these banks suffered **bank runs,** in which large numbers of customers simultaneously withdrew their deposits, and some ultimately failed as a result. The banking panic soon spread more widely, threatening the security of the entire financial system. It was eventually halted only when the famed financier J.P. Morgan induced a large number of banks to join a consortium and mutually stand behind each other's financial obligations.

BIRTH OF THE FED

The Panic of 1907 achieved notoriety at the time by causing the recession of 1907–1908, but the panic's longer-term importance lies elsewhere. Hoping to avoid a repeat of 1907's financial meltdown, Congress in 1913 established the **Federal Reserve System,** commonly referred to as the **Fed.** The Fed is now the nation's monetary authority and, among other things, our first line of defense against financial panics.

As had been true in prior financial panics, the crux of many banks' woes in 1907 was their inability to convert their assets into the cash that panicked depositors desperately wanted. So the Fed was created to serve as "lender of last resort" to the nation's **commercial banks.** Congress empowered the Fed to lend funds to banks to meet whatever demands that depositors put on the banks, regardless of how great those demands might be. The intention was that there would never be another financial panic in the United States, an objective that, if achieved, would significantly reduce the number and severity of the nation's economic **recessions.**

OPPORTUNITY AND FAILURE

The Fed's first real chance to perform as lender of last resort—the function for which it was created—came in 1930 when several prominent New York banks got into financial difficulties. Customers of those and other banks started withdrawing funds, fearing that their banks might be weak. This spreading lack of confidence was exactly the scenario the Fed was created to defend against—yet it did nothing. The result was a banking panic and a worsening of the economic downturn already under way.

The next year, the Fed had two more opportunities to act as lender of last resort when confidence in banks sagged, yet in both cases it again failed to act. The results were recurring bank panics in 1931 and an intensification of what was by then an extremely severe recession. Early in 1933, eroding public confidence in the banking system gave the Fed yet another opportunity to step in as lender of last resort, and *again* it failed to do so. The resulting banking panic was disastrous and ushered in the deepest stages of what has come to be known as the Great Depression. It is little wonder that Herbert Hoover, who was then president of the United States, referred to the Fed as "a weak reed for a nation to lean on in time of trouble."

LESSONS LEARNED

Thirty years after the end of the Great Depression, Nobel laureate Milton Friedman and Anna Schwartz published *A Monetary History of the United States.* Among other things, this book laid out in detail the story of the Fed's failings during the 1930s. The book's lessons were absorbed by at least two people who have since served as the head of the Fed— Alan Greenspan, who was chair of the Fed from 1987 to 2006, and Ben Bernanke, who succeeded Greenspan.

Greenspan's opportunity to have the Fed serve as the banking system's lender of last resort came in September 2001, in the wake of the terrorist attacks on the World Trade Center towers. Banks found themselves in need of a quick infusion of funds as panicked depositors made large-scale withdrawals of cash. The Fed quickly stepped in to provide funds to banks, enabling them to meet the demands of depositors without having to sell off **assets** quickly at depressed prices. A terrorist attack surely had never been contemplated by the legislators who created the Fed. Nevertheless, the Fed acted vigorously as a lender of last resort and thus achieved the objectives of its creators—prevention of financial panic.

THE PANIC OF 2008

Only two years after he replaced Greenspan as chair of the Fed, Ben Bernanke had an even bigger opportunity to put the Fed to work. Late in 2008, rapidly eroding confidence in the U.S. financial system led to the near or total collapse of several major financial firms. Many commercial banks, investment banks, and even insurance companies were suddenly in dire condition. Potential borrowers across the country found themselves unable to obtain funds from anyone, at any rate of interest. Although circumstances differed from 1907 in that commercial banks were not at the center of the panic, there was no doubt about one point: The Panic of 2008 was just as threatening to the U.S. economy as its century-old predecessor had been.

Mindful of the costs of inaction, the Fed moved swiftly to maintain and restore confidence in key components of the financial system. But its actions were considerably broader than ever before. Historically, for example, the Fed has lent funds to commercial banks and to the federal government itself. But in 2008, the Fed also lent hundreds of billions of dollars directly to nonbank corporations around the country, including tens of billions to insurance giant AIG. The Fed also began purchasing obligations of government-sponsored **mortgage** market giants Fannie Mae and Freddie Mac, hoping to bolster their solvency. And finally, the Fed agreed to the following trade with commercial banks: It would exchange billions of dollars of risk-free federal **bonds** it held for billions of dollars of high-risk private bonds that they held. In effect, the Fed helped the banks remove high-risk assets of questionable value from their **balance sheets,** thus reducing the chances that skittish depositors might suddenly make large-scale withdrawals of funds from commercial banks.

THE SURGE IN EXCESS RESERVES

On many of their deposits, commercial banks are required to keep a minimum amount of **reserves** on hand, either in their vaults or on deposit with the Fed. These are referred to as **required reserves.** Any reserves above these minimum required levels are called **excess reserves.** Over the past seventy years, bank holdings of excess reserves generally have been quite small, amounting to no more than a few billion dollars for the entire banking system. This is not surprising. In normal times, banks generally keep only enough excess reserves to handle day-to-day transactions with depositors, because they can earn interest on any funds they lend out.

By 2009, excess reserves had soared to more than $800 billion, and in 2011 hit $1.6 *trillion.* Total reserves (required plus excess) were up sharply because the Fed was providing banks reserves in return for other assets. Among the purchases were commercial paper (debts issued by private companies), securities backed by credit card debt and home mortgages, and even home mortgages themselves. But almost all of the Fed-provided reserves simply sat there—either in bank vaults or on deposit with the Fed—because banks lent almost none of them out.

Banks across the country held on to the excess reserves for three reasons. First, the sagging economy meant that borrowers were riskier and hence less profitable at any given interest rate. Second, depositors were greatly concerned about the financial condition of commercial banks. The banks therefore wanted plenty of funds on hand—in the form of excess reserves—in case they had to meet increased withdrawal demands by depositors. Oddly enough, the third reason for the failure of banks to lend out reserves was a new policy implemented by the Fed itself.

Paying Interest on Reserves

In 2008, the Fed began paying interest on the reserves held by commercial banks, something it had never done before. And it was paying interest not just on required reserves but on *excess* reserves as well. This policy encouraged banks to hold excess reserves rather than to lend the funds to customers. Thus, the payment of interest on commercial bank reserves made it *more difficult* for companies and individuals to get loans. (See Chapter 20 for more on this.)

On balance, it remains to be seen whether the Fed actions during the last recession lived up to the expectations that the Fed's founders had more than a century ago. By providing funds to banks and other financial institutions, the Fed helped reduce the impact of the financial panic and helped prevent widespread runs on commercial banks. Nevertheless, the Fed decision to pay interest on reserves markedly discouraged banks from lending those reserves to companies and households across the land. This surely *slowed* recovery from the recession. Only time and further study will tell whether, on balance, the Fed's actions during the recession made us better off—or worse off.

FOR CRITICAL ANALYSIS

1. How did the Fed's long-standing policy of not paying interest on bank reserves act much like a tax on bank reserves?

2. If the Fed continued to pay interest on required reserves but stopped paying interest on excess reserves, how would bank lending incentives be changed?

3. If the Fed had not injected reserves into the banking system in 2008, what would have been the consequences for the banks and for **aggregate demand**?

4. By late 2010 concerns over bank solvency had faded. How did this change likely alter the incentives of banks to lend out excess reserves? What are the implications for aggregate demand? Explain.

5. In the long run, if the Fed fails to remove the excess reserves from the banking system, what will the banks do with them? What are the implications for inflation? Explain.

6. The Fed was given great power in 1913 to undertake potentially beneficial actions. Did this also give it great power to engage in potentially *harmful* actions? Explain why or why not.

CHAPTER 20

The Fed Feeding Frenzy

"QE1 didn't seem to work. QE2 fared little better. Wonder what QE3 will bring."

If you have no idea what the above quote means, you are not alone. Here is the origin of the abbreviation "QE." Financial reporters decided a few years ago to accept a new term for what is largely an old concept. That term is **quantitative easing (QE).** Consequently, "QE1" is a reference to the Fed's expansionary monetary policy during the latest serious recession, in 2008 and 2009. QE2 refers to the Fed's expansionary monetary policy that started in November 2010. QE3—well, the Fed started that in September, 2012, with the economy still moving sideways.

Monetary Policy—The Way It Used to Be

Historically, the Fed's main tool for monetary policy has been the purchase and sale of U.S. government securities, usually **Treasury bills.** When the Fed has wanted to engage in expansionary monetary policy, it bought U.S. Treasuries in the **open market,** thereby increasing **reserves** in the banking system. **Excess reserves** (those over and above legally **required reserves**) were used by banks to expand loans. In the process, the **money supply** grew, which increased aggregate demand. Contractionary monetary policy was just the opposite—the Fed sold U.S. government securities, thereby reducing reserves. The end result was a decrease in the money supply in circulation and a decrease in aggregate demand.

That was then, but the Fed's ordinary monetary policy took on a new twist in response to the financial panic of 2008.

THE FED STARTED TO LIKE OTHER ASSETS

During the first 95 years of its existence, the Federal Reserve dealt with U.S. government securities only. All that changed in 2008 when the Fed decided that it had to target specific sectors in our economy. So, instead of engaging in traditional expansionary monetary policy, the Fed started buying assets other than U.S. government securities. This was something that had never been done before.

The assets purchased by the Fed included (and still include) short-term corporate debt, short-term loans to banks, **mortgage-backed securities,** mostly issued by the government-sponsored corporations Fannie Mae and Freddie Mac, other debt issued by Fannie Mae and Freddie Mac, and preferred shares in the former investment bank Bear Stearns and in the insurance company American International Group (AIG). Oh, and let's not forget that for well over a year the Fed engaged in **foreign currency swaps** with other countries—perhaps that was considered the icing on the larger cake.

All of those purchases of all of those assets clearly increased the size and composition of the Fed's **balance sheet.** For much of its more recent existence, the Fed "owned" anywhere from several billion to several hundred billion dollars of U.S. Treasury securities. But by 2011, the Fed's assets totaled more than $2.5 trillion (including many hundreds of billions in "new" securities it had bought as part of its quantitative easing policy). Throughout 2012 and 2013, Fed assets remained in the range $2.8 to $3.0 trillion.

So, in a sentence, the Fed's traditional monetary policy abruptly changed in 2008. Rather than seeking to stimulate the entire economy in general, the Fed decided to provide credit to parts of financial markets (and even specific corporations) that it believed were being abandoned by private lenders. Never before in its history had the chair of the Fed and its board of directors used such discretionary policy to benefit specific sectors of the economy.

WHY WASN'T THERE AN OUTBREAK OF INFLATION?

When the Fed aggressively adds to the money supply in circulation by buying U.S. government securities, the banking system suddenly has excess reserves. Not wanting to lose out on potential income from those excess reserves, depository institutions increase their loans, the money supply rises, and aggregate demand increases. At least that is the way economists used to tell the story.

While QE1, QE2, and so forth got the headlines, however, there was a revolution in central banking in the United States. Starting on October 1, 2008, the Fed began paying interest on reserves—*all* reserves, including excess reserves. While some monetary economists for years have argued that interest should be paid on required reserves, none ever demanded that interest be paid on excess reserves, too. This policy change by the Fed converted excess reserves into an income-earning asset for banks, and thus fundamentally altered the nature of the conduct of monetary policy.

If you are the manager of a bank and know that the Fed will pay interest on excess reserves, you are not so keen to loan out those reserves to businesses and individuals. After all, if you make loans to businesses and individuals, you run a risk. During the recession of 2007–2009, that risk appeared to be much greater than normal. Why not just sit back, collect interest checks from the U.S. government on all of your reserves and wait to see what happens?

Well, that is exactly how most banks have proceeded over the past few years. The numbers tell the story. When they did not earn interest, excess reserves were a drag on bank profits and so banks kept them to a minimum. Typically, excess reserves for the entire banking system averaged $2–$3 billion. During 2011 they peaked at over $1.6 *trillion* and since then have routinely stayed above $1.0 trillion. Thus, most of the reserves injected into the banking system since 2008 have ended up not in new loans, new money, and new spending. Instead, they ended up sitting in the form of new excess reserves. That means that the "expansionary" quantitative easing of the Fed was almost completely offset by its decision to pay interest on excess reserves. The result was little increase in aggregate demand and little upward pressure on inflation—at least in the short run.

ON WANTING MORE INFLATION

For several years, the Fed has told reporters and experts alike that it was worried about **deflation.** Deflation has been associated with bad times—the Great Depression in the United States, for example, and the "lost decade" of the 1990s in the Japanese economy. In justification of its quantitative easing (QE2) in November 2010, the Fed pointed to the "need" for a little bit of inflation, to avoid a deflationary downward spiral.

Actually, as measured by the personal consumption expenditures (PCE) price index, there had been inflation running at about 1.2 percent annually, a number that was bumping up around 2 percent toward the end of 2010, when the Fed announced QE2. In other words, based on the Fed's historically preferred price index, there was no sign of deflation, so it seemed strange that the Fed argued in favor of quantitative easing to avoid deflation. The source of the Fed's deflation worries is easily identified, though. Without much publicity, in 2010 the Fed switched from the personal consumption expenditure price index to the consumer price index (CPI) as its preferred measure of inflation. The CPI gives almost double the weight to housing prices than does the personal consumption expenditure price index. Given that housing prices fell quite dramatically during the years 2006–2010, it is not surprising that the CPI showed some deflation, especially in 2008.

Getting Back to Quantitative Easing

Even if the Fed's argument about deflation was based on no more than a switch in price indexes, its desire to prime the pump for the faltering U.S. economy is genuine. The recession that started in December 2007 pushed the unemployment rate above 10 percent, and the rate was slow to drop back below 9 percent. So the Fed argued that QE2 would lower long-term interest rates and thereby give the economy a boost. QE3 was similarly justified on the ground that the unemployment rate had been slow to drop below 8 percent.

When the Fed buys up government and other debt obligations, it will push investors into stocks and corporate bonds—raising the latter's values and lowering interest rates. Lower borrowing costs should help some homeowners refinance their mortgages. Some businesses will be helped, too, because they will have access to cheaper credit. Such analysis is quite traditional and at times has worked—*in the short run*. In the long run, in contrast, large-scale purchases of debt, whether labeled quantitative easing or not, will simply lead to more rapid growth in the money supply, a higher rate of inflation and a return of interest rates to their previous and even higher levels.

So, the Fed might well be thought of as being on a tightrope of its own making. The huge infusion of reserves into the banking system helped moderate the recession of 2007–2009, but the payment of interest on reserves slowed the recovery from that recession. The presence of large excess reserves presents a huge potential threat of inflation down the road, but if the reserves are pulled out of the banking system too fast, the economy will surely sink back into recession. It is the classic case of the two-handed economic policy problem. On the one hand, the economy is threatened by severe inflation. On the other hand, it is threatened by a relapse into recession. Stay tuned, for this is one drama that will work itself out in front of your very eyes.

FOR CRITICAL ANALYSIS

1. Why do increases in the money supply in circulation ultimately lead to inflation?

2. Was the Fed justified in targeting specific sectors of the economy during the financial panic of 2008? Why or why not?

3. When the Fed buys U.S. government securities, how does it pay for them?

4. Is there any risk to the Fed in holding mortgage-backed securities and debt issued by Fannie Mae and Freddie Mac? If so, what is it?

5. Why did excess reserves increase so much in recent years?

6. Why have banks been so reluctant to loan funds to businesses in recent years?

CHAPTER 21

Deposit Insurance and Financial Markets

During the Panic of 2008, the federal government announced a key new policy: It was insuring against loss all bank deposits up to $250,000 per account. Thus, if your depository institution happened to be holding some toxic (possibly even worthless) **mortgage-backed securities,** you were home free. The bank could suffer terrible losses, even go out of business, and yet your accounts, up to $250,000 each, would be guaranteed by the full faith and of the U.S. government—which is to say, the U.S. taxpayer.

If you happened to notice the announcement of this policy, you may have wondered to yourself, why would the government do this? For example, although the federal government bought **shares of stock** in numerous banks at the same time, it most assuredly does not guarantee the value of those shares. Why treat deposits differently? A more subtle question is this: How do banks and other **depository institutions** behave differently because of this special deposit insurance? And you might even have wondered whether *your* behavior is likely to be any different because of this insurance. To get a handle on these and other questions, we must look back to the 1930s, before the notion of deposit insurance had even been conceived.

Runs on Banks

Bank runs are defined as the simultaneous rush of depositors to convert their deposits into **currency.** Until the federal government set up deposit insurance in 1933, runs on banks were an infrequent but seemingly unavoidable occurrence, sometimes becoming widespread during economic **recessions.** The largest number of bank runs in modern history occurred during the Great Depression. As a result, more than *nine thousand* banks failed during the 1930s.

Just put yourself in the shoes of the depositor in a typical bank in 1930 and remember that you are a **creditor** of the bank. That is to say, your deposits in the bank are its **liabilities.** Suppose a rumor develops that the **assets** of the bank are not sufficient to cover its liabilities. In other words, the bank is, or will soon be, **insolvent.** Presumably, you are worried that you will not get your deposits back in the form of currency. Knowing this, you are likely to rush to the bank. All other depositors who hear about the bank's supposedly weak financial condition are likely to do the same thing.

This is the essence of a bank run: Regardless of the true state of the bank's financial condition, rumors or fears that a bank is in trouble can cause depositors to suddenly attempt to withdraw all of their funds. But many assets of a bank are in the form of loans that cannot immediately be converted into cash. Even if **solvent**, the bank is said to be **illiquid** because it does not have enough cash on hand to meet the demands of fearful depositors. And when it attempts to get that cash by selling some assets, any resulting decline in the market value of those assets can quickly turn a solvent bank into an insolvent one.

Bank runs can be disastrous for the economy because when they occur, the nation's **money supply** shrinks as people pull cash out of banks and stuff it under their mattresses (or wherever they think it might be safe). This in turn causes **aggregate demand** to fall, leading to higher unemployment, business failures, and yet more concerns for the solvency of banks. Quickly enough, the result can be an economic recession and widespread hardship.

Deposit Insurance

When bank failures hit 4,000 in 1933, the federal government decided to act to prevent further bank runs. That year, Congress passed, and the president signed into law, legislation creating the Federal Deposit Insurance Corporation (FDIC) and the next year created the Federal Savings and Loan Insurance Corporation (FSLIC). Many years later, in 1971, the National Credit Union Share Insurance Fund (NCUSIF) was created to insure credit union deposits, and in 1989, the FSLIC was replaced by the Savings Association Insurance Fund (SAIF). To make our discussion simple, we will focus only on the FDIC, but the general principles apply to all of these agencies.

When the FDIC was formed, it insured each account in a commercial bank against a loss of up to $2,500. That figure has been increased on seven different occasions, reaching $250,000 in 2008. The result of federal deposit insurance is that there has not been a widespread bank run in the United States since the Great Depression, despite numerous bank failures in the interim. Even during the Panic of 2008, when confidence in many financial institutions collapsed, federally insured depository institutions continued to operate. Indeed, total deposits in them actually rose. The good news about federal deposit insurance is that it has prevented bank runs. But this has come at a significant cost, arising largely due to the unintended consequences of deposit insurance.

ADVERSE SELECTION

Suppose someone offers you what is claimed to be a great **investment** opportunity. That person tells you that if you invest $250,000, you will make a very high rate of return, say, 20 percent per year, much higher than the 3 percent your funds are currently earning elsewhere. No matter how much you trusted the person offering you this deal, you would probably do some serious investigation of the proposed investment before you handed over all of these hard-earned dollars. You, like other people, would carefully evaluate the risk factors involved in this potential opportunity.

For example, if you use part of your **savings** to buy a house, you will undoubtedly have the structural aspects of the house checked out by an inspector before you sign on the dotted line. Similarly, if you planned to purchase an expensive piece of art, you surely would have an independent expert verify that the artwork is authentic. Typically, the same is true every time you place your accumulated savings into any potential investment: You look before you leap. In circumstances such as these, there is initially **asymmetric information**—in this case, the seller knows much more than the potential buyer. But with diligence, the buyer can eliminate much of this gap in knowledge and make a wise decision.

Now ask yourself, when is the last time you examined the financial condition or lending activities of the depository institution at which you have your checking or savings account? We predict that the answer is never. Indeed, why should you investigate? Because of federal deposit insurance, you know that even if the depository institution that has your funds is taking big risks, you are personally risking nothing. If that depository institution fails, the federal government will—with 100 percent certainty—make sure that you get 100 percent of your deposits back, up to the insurance limit.

So here we have it, the first unintended consequence of depository insurance. Depositors like you no longer have any substantial incentive to investigate the track record of the owners or managers of banks.

You care little about whether they have a history of risky or imprudent behavior because at worst you may suffer some minor inconvenience if your bank fails. Thus, unlike in the days before deposit insurance, the marketplace today does little to monitor or punish past performance of owners or managers of depository institutions. As a result, we tend to get **adverse selection**—instead of banks owned and operated by individuals who are prudent at making careful decisions on behalf of depositors, many of them end up run by people who have a high tolerance for taking big risks with other people's money.

MORAL HAZARD

Now let's look at bank managers' incentives to act cautiously when making loans. You must first note that the riskier the loan, the higher the interest rate that a bank can charge. For example, if a developing country with a blemished track record in paying its debts wishes to borrow from a U.S. depository institution, that country will have to pay a much higher interest rate than a less risky debtor. The same is true when a risky company comes looking for a loan: If it gets one at all, it will be at a higher-than-average interest rate.

When trying to decide which loan applicants should receive funds, bank managers must weigh the trade-off between risk and return. Poor credit risks offer high **profits** if they actually pay off their debts, but good credit risks are more likely to pay off their debts. The right choice means higher profits for the bank and likely higher salaries and promotions for the managers. The wrong choice means losses and perhaps insolvency for the bank and new, less desirable careers for the managers.

To understand how bank mangers' incentives are changed by deposit insurance—even for managers who otherwise would be prudent and conservative—consider two separate scenarios. In the first scenario, the bank manager is told to take $250,000 of depositors' funds to Las Vegas. The rules of the game are that the manager can bet however he or she wants, and the bank will *share* the winnings *and losses* equally with the deposit holders whose funds the manager has in trust. In the second scenario, the same bank manager with the same funds is given a different set of rules. In this case, the bank does not have to share in any of the losses, but it will share in any of the gains when betting in Las Vegas.

Under which set of rules do you think the bank manager will take the higher risks while betting in Las Vegas? Clearly, the manager will take higher risks in the second scenario because the bank will not suffer at all if the manager loses the entire $250,000. Yet if the manager hits it big, say, by placing a successful bet on double zero in roulette, the bank will share the profits, and the manager is likely to get a raise and a promotion.

Well, the second scenario is exactly the one facing the managers of federally insured depository institutions. If they make risky loans, thereby earning, at least in the short run, higher profits, they share in the "winnings." The result for them is higher salaries. If, by contrast, some of these risky loans are not repaid, what is the likely outcome? The bank's losses are limited because the federal government (which is to say you, the taxpayer) will cover any shortfall between the bank's assets and its liabilities. Thus, federal deposit insurance means that banks get to enjoy all of the profits of risk without bearing all of the consequences of that risk.

So the second unintended consequence of deposit insurance is to encourage **moral hazard.** Specifically, bank managers of all types (risk lovers or not) have an incentive to take higher risks in their lending policies than they otherwise would. Indeed, when the economy turned down in the early 1980s, we got to see the consequences of exactly this change in incentives. From 1985 to the beginning of 1993, a total of 1,065 depository institutions failed, at an average rate of more than ten times that for the preceding forty years. The losses from these failures totaled billions of dollars—paid for in large part by you, the taxpayer.

What, then, might be expected from the 2008 insurance hike to $250,000? Well, in the short run, confidence in banks was renewed and depositors were encouraged to keep more funds in banks. This was good news, for it helped the economy adjust to the financial shocks of 2008–2009. But the bad news will be forthcoming in the long run: The higher deposit insurance limits will encourage both adverse selection (more risk-loving bank managers) and moral hazard (more risk taking by bank managers of all stripes). Eventually, the lending standards of banks will deteriorate to the point that losses mount once again—paid for in part by you, the taxpayer.

Paying for Deposit Insurance

For the first sixty years or so of federal deposit insurance, all depository institutions were charged modest fees for their insurance coverage. Unfortunately, the fee that these depository institutions paid was completely unrelated to the riskiness of the loans they made. A bank that made loans to Microsoft was charged the same rate for deposit insurance as a bank that made loans to a start-up company with no track record whatsoever. Hence, not even the fees paid by banks for their insurance gave them any incentive to be prudent. This is completely unlike the case in private insurance markets, in which high-risk customers are charged higher premiums, giving them at least some incentive to become lower-risk customers.

In the early 1990s, the federal government made a feeble attempt to adjust fees for depository insurance to reflect the riskiness of their lending activities. But the political strength of the depository institutions prevented any fundamental change in the system. In 2008, the insurance fees paid by depository institutions were doubled, but even this was not enough to keep up with the added risks of the higher insurance limits. In 2009 the insurance rules were changed again. There are now four basic risk categories for banks, with different insurance premiums charged in each category. In addition, there is a separate set of rules and premiums that apply to what the FDIC calls "large and highly complex institutions." Although this multitiered arrangement is an improvement on the past, most experts believe that it still does not adequately charge banks for the risks they impose on the insurance system. That is, the premiums are not nearly enough to cover the likely losses of the riskiest banks or enough to get them to change their risky behavior.

So while your banker is headed to Vegas, you'd better plan on staying at home to work. Sooner or later, as a U.S. taxpayer, your bill for deposit insurance will come due.

FOR CRITICAL ANALYSIS

1. If federal deposit insurance costs nothing, who pays when an insured depository institution fails and its depositors are nonetheless reimbursed for the full amount of their deposits?

2. In a world without deposit insurance, what are some of the mechanisms that would arise to "punish" bank managers who acted irresponsibly? (*Hint:* There are similar types of mechanisms for consumer goods and in the stock market.)

3. Explain how "experience rating" of insurance—charging higher premiums to higher-risk customers—affects the incidence of both adverse selection and moral hazard.

4. Why doesn't the federal government fully price bank failure risks?

5. How would the chance of a major economic depression change if federal deposit insurance were eliminated?

6. Why doesn't the federal government offer automobile accident insurance?

CHAPTER 22

Phone It In: The Coming Revolution in the Payments System

Dollars, quarters, dimes, nickels, pennies, credit cards, debit cards, and don't forget about checks. And there is something called wire transfers between banks. Everything just listed in one way or another makes up our **payments system.** Sometimes we use the quaint items we call **currency**—bill and coins. At other times we use soon-to-become quaint credit cards. And for most young people, checks appear quite strange indeed, for the youth of today are used to debit cards. Massive computing power, the Internet, and the communications revolution, however, are about to change how all of us pay for what we buy.

CURRENCY AND COINS—A THING OF THE PAST?

For those who want to work "off the books" (to avoid paying income taxes) and those who are engaged in illegal drug trafficking, currency conveniently leaves no electronic trail. But currency also has lots of disadvantages, whoever uses it. If you lose your wallet or purse, you are certain to lose your currency. If you want to pay for something in cash, unless it involves a very small amount, currency is awkward (and can become heavy).

Using coins is even more of a bother. And certainly today in the United States and elsewhere, most coins cannot buy you much at all. Plus, it costs 2.4 cents to produce one U.S. penny and 11.2 cents to produce one nickel. In 2012, Canada finally got rid of its pennies, which had been around since 1858. In Britain, the farthing was worth one-quarter of an old penny. Nonetheless, it remained **legal tender** for 700 years before it was retired from circulation in 1960. Although coins last fifty times as long as paper currency, they are heavy and awkward. Once a coin is no longer usable to buy an item, it is living on borrowed time. Once upon a time, a penny would get you an ice cream cone. Today, there is little reason to keep it in circulation.

Retailers often price goods at $9.99 or $14.99. That custom was started to avoid fraud. Employees are forced to open the cash register to provide change. Because most customers use debit or credit cards today, the .99 is superfluous, though. But the major reason that coins and bills are going to disappear has to do with the move to electronic money. Besides, right now about 60 percent of U.S. dollars are used outside the United States anyway.

We Should Cheer for Falling Computing Costs

Before we describe the coming electronic payments revolution, we need first to understand why it has become possible. The "why" of course involves the falling costs of computing. Consider that in 1991, a megabyte of memory was priced at $50. If nothing had changed since then, a typical 32-gigabyte smartphone would cost about $1,000,000. But the price of memory has fallen dramatically. Even ten years ago, a smartphone with 32 gigs would have cost $10,000. Since then, of course, the market for smartphones has exploded. Not only has the price of memory plunged, so too has the cost of producing smartphones. (Smartphone and tablet device manufacturers have been able to take advantage of **economies of scale**.) And it has helped that smartphones are now not much larger than the simplest cell phones.

Along with fast and cheap computing with smartphones and tablet devices, the spread of the Internet and its growing speed have improved, too. Does anybody remember dial-up? Does anyone remember when it would take a whole day to download one movie? Internet speeds and availability of networks have improved so much that we take fast access on our smartphones and tablet devices for granted. Oh, did we mention the millions of Wi-Fi hotspots throughout the world? A decade ago, such "necessities" would have been dreams of pure fantasy, but not today.

The Apps Revolution and Starbucks

Where there are smartphones and tablet devices, there are apps, and not just a few of them, but hundreds of thousands, and maybe even millions. As smartphones and tablets have become almost ubiquitous, particularly among young people, application developers have created an astounding array of downloadable apps. Each new generation of smartphones also has more apps built in.

Not surprisingly, the possibility of creating apps for electronic payment systems has intrigued the banking and business world for years. The first payment apps have involved fairly standard (at least now) technology. Consider the example of Starbucks. A few years ago, Starbucks teamed up with Square, a then-small online payment system start-up in San Francisco. After you download a Square app onto your smartphone, Starbucks can use the Square barcode to "capture" just the right amount of electronic money from your credit card account to pay for your $5 cappuccino.

The E-Wallet—Holy Grail of Payment Systems

Eventually, having a barcode app on one's smartphone will seem quite old fashioned. What big retailers, big banks, Google, Microsoft, and Apple all want is something more sophisticated called an **e-wallet**. An e-wallet is just that—it acts as does a real wallet, but it is embedded in your smartphone or tablet device. Just as you have currency in your wallet, you can already have the equivalent of currency in certain e-wallets that are functioning today.

For e-wallets to really be effective, they must be able to transmit to an e-cash register in a store. To do so requires **near-field communication (NFC)**. This is the technology that enables radio communication between smartphones and other devices that are close by—without actually touching the device. Most NFC systems involve common radio frequency identification (RFID) technology, which can be made quite secure.

The lack of NFC chips in current smartphones has slowed down the movement toward true e-wallets. Because major retailers have not yet set up systems for e-wallets in North America, only about 10 million smartphones sold in 2012 had the NFC technology embedded. There are rumors that Apple will include the NFC chip in all of its future iPads and iPhones. The same may be true for Google's tablet devices and Nokia's Windows phones.

The Competition Is Fierce, but Scattered

The number of e-wallet systems being put into the marketplace is accelerating. One mobile payment option is called Tabbedout. In 2012, T.G.I. Fridays was the first national chain of restaurants to incorporate this mobile payment option. After ordering from a server, diners with Tabbedout apps can pay their bills using their credit card on file when they leave. The number of T.G.I. Fridays accepting the system is still under 1000, though.

AT&T Mobility, T-Mobile, and Verizon teamed up to create Isis SmartTap. This new payment system has been installed in numerous gas pumps throughout the United States. Google has created its own Google Wallet and is expanding its use at a rapid pace. Wal-Mart, Target, and Japan's 7-Eleven created the Merchant Customer Exchange, or MCX, which resembles a Google Wallet. Both systems allow users to store credit cards, gift cards, sales promotions, and loyalty cards on their app, and then pay with the greatest of ease.

Just Sit Back, Watch TV, and Spend

If you ever look at TV (and we know that fewer and fewer college students do), you will find that there are shopping channels for which you can call in, give your credit card, and buy certain items. There are, particularly on late-night and very early morning shows, ads for items such as steak knives that can cut through steel and spray sealants that will float a boat made out of screen doors. You can pay for all of these wondrous items simply by calling an 800 number and reading out your credit card information.

The payment service PayPal has decided to make it even easier for you to buy when watching your TV. The company has created a joint venture with the cable company Comcast and with the set-top-maker TiVo to allow TV viewers to use their remote controls to buy goods. The system also allows viewers to donate to various charities that advertise on TV, again by using just the remote control. Provided you have a PayPal account—and there are a hundred million people who do—under certain circumstances you can click on TV commercials to make your purchases or provide donations to nonprofits and political campaigns. You can even ask advertisers to text you information on your smartphones.

The Technology Is There, but It Is Not Uniform

Imagine that the local pizza hangout only accepted Visa credit cards that were circular in shape. Assume also that your local smartphone store only accepted American Express cards that had triangular shapes. You get the picture. If that were the case, you would have to have one heck of a lot of different credit cards (or debit cards as the case might be). Many years ago, however, credit card companies set up a common system using a common-sized card with, at least in the United States, common magnetic stripes on the back. In other words, there are agreed-upon standards.

Well, today, for e-wallets and similar payment systems, companies have not yet settled on the best ways to do things, so it is similar to an era of circular and triangular credit cards. Until at least the biggest of the mobile payment players agree on common technology standards and a platform on which to implement them, mobile payments simply will not work across all wireless networks, digital devices, credit card types, and retailers.

Have no fear, an agreement will come. Trillions of dollars of transactions occur every month throughout the world, so the payoff to finding a common technology for smartphone payments is huge. Everyone wants a piece of the big pie. The phone companies want in, the credit card companies of course want to be there, and the giant tech companies see billions of dollars in their future. And this means cash is doomed.

Retailers see something else, besides ease of payment and relief from the burden of handling currency and coins.

Bringing Back the Small-Store Experience

Way back when, all shopping was done face-to-face in small-store environments. Often as not, the retailer knew all of her or his customers. Customers could ask their friendly general goods store owner for advice. E-wallets may bring back a semblance of such customer-retailer relationships. Why? Because eventually e-wallets will allow for the following:

1. A place where loyalty cards can be kept, but electronically.

2. A comparison-shopping tool.

3. A way to alert a retailer that you have walked in the store so that she can recommend products based on your previous purchases.

4. A presentation of reviews of the products you are looking at while you are looking at them.

And more!

It will not be quite as close-up and personal as in "mom and pop stores," but perhaps it is the best we can hope for in our expanding technological shopping world. Besides, it means only one wallet to lug around, and an in-store shopping experience with all the bells and whistles of being online. Of course, you will still have to change out of your pajamas to go shopping.

For Critical Analysis

1. Why might it be a mistake for a uniform technology standard to be imposed in today's payment systems?

2. What are the downsides of loading an e-wallet into your smartphone or tablet device?

3. What are the upsides for retailers of a smartphone payments system?

4. Will anyone be worse off? (*Hint*: Think armored trucks and Brinks.)

5. What is the downside, even with a fully functional e-wallet system in place, of never carrying any cash with you?

6. What is the difference between preloaded cash cards offered by, for example, American Express, and e-wallets?

PART FIVE

Globalization and International Finance

CHAPTER 23

The Value of the Dollar

When the euro was introduced in 1999, you could purchase one for $1.18. Three years later, when euro banknotes and coins began circulating as the monetary unit of most of the **European Union (EU),** the market price of the euro had fallen to $0.90. Since then, the euro's price has fluctuated between $0.86 and $1.70. This pattern of fluctuating prices is not unique to the euro. In a world of **flexible exchange rates,** the prices at which different **currencies** trade for each other are determined by the forces of world **demand** and **supply.** Thus, if the demand for euros rises, its price will rise, and if its demand falls, so too will its price. And what is true for the euro is just as true for the British pound sterling, the Japanese yen, and our very own U.S. dollar. As we shall see, these changes in market forces, and the resulting changes in **exchange rates,** play a key role in determining patterns of international trade.

SOME TERMINOLOGY

Although we referred to the dollar price of the euro, we could just as well have talked of the euro price of the dollar. Thus, if it takes $1.25 to purchase a euro, it must also be true that a dollar buys less than a euro. In fact, it buys exactly 1/1.25 euros in this example. That is, the euro price of the dollar is €0.80 (where € is the symbol for the euro). The exchange rate between the two currencies can be expressed either way, although in the United States people usually refer to the exchange rate as the dollar price of foreign currency, and so too shall we. In this example, the exchange rate between the dollar and the euro is thus $1.25.

You will also hear some people, especially journalists and politicians, talk about a "stronger" or "weaker" dollar, accompanied by pronouncements that one or the other condition is good for the United States. When people say the dollar has gotten "stronger," what they mean is that one dollar will buy more units of foreign currency than it used to. Hence, a reduction in the exchange rate from, say, $1.25 to $1.20 per euro amounts to a stronger dollar. Conversely, if the dollar price of the euro rises from $1.25 to $1.35, this would mean that the dollar was weaker because one dollar would buy fewer euros.

GOOD NEWS OR BAD?

Is a weaker dollar good news or bad? Like most value judgments (notice the words *good* and *bad*), the answer is in the eye of the beholder. Suppose the price of the euro rises from $1.25 to $1.50. We say that the dollar has gotten weaker relative to the euro because people must pay more dollars for each euro. Because American consumers must eventually come up with euros if they want to buy French wine or Italian pasta, when the euro becomes more expensive, European goods become more expensive for American consumers.[1] Thus, from the perspective of American consumers, a weak dollar is bad news.

But producers in the United States may have a different view of the world. For example, automobile manufacturers with plants in the United States compete with manufacturers that have European facilities. When the dollar price of the euro rises, so does the dollar price of cars made in Europe. This induces some American consumers to "buy American," which is surely good news for the companies that receive their business. Similarly, recall that the *rise* in the price of the euro is equivalent to a *fall* in the price of the dollar. Such a move in the exchange rate makes American-made goods cheaper abroad. As a result, foreign consumers are also more likely to "buy American," again good news for the companies from whom they purchase. Thus, a weaker dollar encourages exports and discourages imports, but whether that is "good" or "bad" news is clearly a matter on which people might reasonably disagree.

Now, what about the consequences of a "stronger" dollar? When the dollar can buy more euros, this means it can also buy more European goods. This clearly benefits American consumers, so we conclude that they like a strong dollar. American producers, however, will have a different take on matters. They will lose business from American customers, who are now more likely to "buy European." In addition, people in the EU will now find American goods more expensive because the dollar is now more expensive. So they will buy fewer American goods and

---

1 Of course, consumers typically do not physically obtain the euros themselves, but the importers who bring the goods in on their behalf must certainly do so.

make more purchases at home. Thus, we conclude that a stronger dollar will encourage imports into the United States and discourage exports from the United States. Presumably, American consumers and producers will have much different opinions on whether this is good news or bad.

PURCHASING POWER PARITY

Of course, exchange rates do not just move around without cause. There are four well-established forces that play key roles in making them what they are. The first of these, which is by far the most important long-run determinant of exchange rates, is called **purchasing power parity (PPP)**. This principle simply states that the relative values of different currencies must ultimately reflect their **purchasing power** in their home countries.

To see how this works, let's consider the United States and Switzerland, which uses the Swiss franc as its currency. Over the past fifty years, the exchange rate between these two currencies has varied between roughly $0.25 and $1.25, that is, by a factor of five. In the 1960s, for example, the exchange rate was near the bottom end of that range, but it has followed a persistent rise until recently, albeit with some ups and downs along the way. The reason the Swiss franc rose in value relative to the U.S. dollar is simple: Typically, the **inflation** rate in Switzerland has been much lower than that in the United States. The amount of goods that American dollars would buy generally has been shrinking, so the Swiss demand for dollars has fallen, even as Americans have tried to unload their depreciating dollars for Swiss francs. Together, these forces helped push the value of the Swiss franc up, and so the exchange rate rose, to $0.40, then $0.70, and then even above $1.00.

This process applies across all countries. When the **price level** rises in country A relative to the price level in country B, people in both nations will switch some of their purchases of goods from country A to country B. This will push down the value of A's currency and push up the value of B's currency. In fact, this tendency is so strong that it will continue until "parity" is reached. If A's price level *rises* 20 percent relative to B's price level, A's currency ultimately will *fall* in value by 20 percent relative to B's currency. It may take a while for this adjustment to work out, and it may be temporarily masked by some of the forces we shall talk about next, but eventually it will happen.

INTEREST RATES

One key reason for wishing to acquire the currency of another nation is that you want to acquire goods produced in that nation. But there is an added reason: You may wish to invest or to lend funds in that nation. For example, suppose you wanted to purchase **bonds** issued by a Canadian corporation. These would be denominated in Canadian dollars (C$), so you would first have to obtain those Canadian dollars before you could purchase the bonds. Given this, it should be apparent that one of the factors influencing your demand for Canadian dollars is the rate of return, or interest rate, on **investments** in Canada, compared to the interest rate on investments elsewhere. The simplest way of putting this is that if interest rates in Canada rise relative to interest rates in the United States, investors will want to move funds from the United States into Canada. That is, there will be a drop in the demand for U.S. dollars and a rise in the demand for Canadian dollars, and so the exchange rate will rise—you will have to give up more U.S. dollars to obtain one Canadian dollar. The U.S. dollar will have become "weaker" against the Canadian currency.

Note that the interest rates we speak of are **real interest rates,** that is, adjusted for any expected inflation. If interest rates rise in Canada because of an increase in the expected inflation rate there, this hardly makes them more attractive to American, European, or Chinese investors. It simply neutralizes the effects of the higher expected inflation. Similarly, we must be careful to compare interest rates on obligations that have the same **default risk.** If the interest rate is high on bonds issued by a Canadian company that is in danger of **bankruptcy,** that higher interest rate simply compensates **bondholders** for the added default risk they face. It does not make those bonds unusually attractive to investors in the United States or elsewhere.

But as long as we are careful to adjust for expected inflation and risk, interest rate differences can sometimes be quite useful in understanding events. For example, during the late nineteenth century, inflation- and risk-adjusted interest rates were higher in the United States than they were in Britain because the United States was rebuilding from the Civil War, settling the West, and industrializing at a rapid rate. All of these factors made the United States a productive place in which to invest. The higher rate of return in the United States made it attractive for British investors to lend funds to American firms, which in turn meant a higher demand for American dollars. As a result, the American dollar was more valuable on world markets than it otherwise would have been.

HARD CURRENCY

If you have ever visited a developing nation, you may have heard people refer to "hard currency." You may even have had them insist you pay for your purchases not with the local currency but with American dollars or euros or even Swiss francs. The reasoning behind this insistence is simple.

In such countries, whatever the *current* state of economic and political affairs, the *future* state of both is often filled with great uncertainty. Perhaps the current government's political support is not too secure. Or there may be the simmering threat of a military-backed coup. Or maybe there is a suspicion that the national government will not be able to finance its future spending with conventional taxes. Should any of these eventualities be realized, the likely result is that the government will resort to printing money as a means of financing its activities, causing future high inflation that will devastate the purchasing power of the local currency. And because the exact timing and magnitude of this outcome are highly uncertain, so is the expected future value of the local currency.

To reduce their risk, people thus try to hold currencies whose value is unlikely to be subject to political vagaries—and these are currencies issued by strong democratic governments, such as those in the United States and the EU. This increases the demand for such currencies and thus tends to set their values in world markets higher than they otherwise would be. The reference to "hard currency" stems from the notion that the purchasing power of such currencies is as stable as a rock—which it is, compared to the local monies that people are trying to avoid holding.

BOEING AND THE BEATLES

The final key factor that helps determine exchange rates is quite simply the relative attractiveness of the goods produced in various nations. Consider the Boeing Corporation, long regarded as the maker of some of the best commercial jet planes in existence. Airlines all over the world purchase billions of dollars' worth of Boeing aircraft every year. To do this, they must acquire U.S. dollars, and their demand for dollars makes the value of the dollar on world markets higher than it otherwise would be.

Of course, the residents of foreign countries have been known to produce some nice products themselves. Many people feel that the best wines come from France, the best ties from Italy, and so forth. And then there are the Beatles, perhaps the most prolific and popular rock group ever, at least measured by worldwide sales of music. When the Beatles hit the music scene in the 1960s, millions of Americans wanted to acquire recordings of their songs. To do so, they first had to acquire pounds sterling (the money used in Britain). This increased the demand for pounds sterling and thus caused the dollar price of the pound to rise in foreign exchange markets. Thus the next time you pay to download music of the British rock group One Direction, you will know that your decision to buy their music has pushed the dollar price of the pound sterling up, even if just by the tiniest of amounts.

For Critical Analysis

1. Although the United Kingdom is a member of the EU, it does not use the euro as its monetary unit. Instead it uses the pound sterling. If the United Kingdom decided to switch from the pound to the euro, how might this decision affect the value of the euro in foreign exchange markets?

2. In an effort to discourage drug smugglers from using U.S. currency in major drug deals, the U.S. government refuses to issue currency in denominations greater than $100. How does this policy decision affect the demand for dollars and thus the exchange rate between the dollar and other currencies, such as the euro (which comes in denominations as big as €500)?

3. Sometimes national governments decide that they do not want their currencies to be any lower in value than they currently are. Explain how, if a country wants to raise the value of its currency in foreign exchange markets, it might use the following tools to do so:

   a. Altering the rate of growth in its money supply, thus changing the current and expected inflation rate

   b. Limiting the ability of citizens to invest in foreign nations

   c. Imposing **tariffs or quotas** on imports

   d. Subsidizing exports by domestic firms

4. From shortly after World War II to the early 1970s, the United States (like many countries) was on a system of fixed exchange rates. That is, the U.S. government pledged to take whatever actions were necessary to keep the value of the dollar fixed relative to other currencies. Consider the emergence of the Beatles in the 1960s. What would the U.S. government have to do to prevent the value of the dollar from changing as a result? Alternatively, consider the introduction of the popular Boeing 707 in the 1950s. What would the U.S. government have to do to prevent the value of the dollar from changing as a result?

5. Why do politicians worry about whether the dollar is "strong" or "weak"?

6. What do you think happened to the value of the U.S. dollar when BMW (a German company) moved an important part of its manufacturing facilities to the United States some years ago? Explain.

CHAPTER **24**

Is the Eurozone Zoning Out?

Here is a fictitious story about the United States. Assume that until fifteen years ago, all fifty states were separate countries with their own separate currencies and their own **central banks.** Assume further that there were no trade restrictions so that goods and services could be exchanged between any two state-countries. Next assume that all fifty got together and agreed to use one currency—the dollar—controlled by one central bank in Washington, D.C. Further assume that all the states signed a formal agreement in which they established that there would be no government transfers of income from one state to another. They also agreed that none of them would run much of a government deficit.

Flash forward fifteen years. Certain states did not "follow the rules." They ended up with huge government deficits because of generous welfare spending, generous pay and pension packages for their government employees, and lavish state building projects. What to do? Just ask all of the other states to help them out because of the **debt crisis** they faced. And why would other states likely help them out? There are two reasons. First, if the states with debt crises do not get help, they will go bankrupt. This will reduce the demand for goods from other states, tending to raise unemployment and lower economic growth. Second, bankruptcies in some states will likely cause other nations around the world to fear even more defaults. This will cause a loss of confidence in the dollar and might even force all of the states to abandon the dollar as their common currency.

Move from Fantasy into European Reality

Of course, the situation just described did not actually happen fifteen years ago in the United States. Rather, it happened in the so-called

Eurozone in Europe. The **European Union (EU)** started decades ago and now has twenty-seven member countries. Seventeen of those countries all use one currency—the **euro.** When the euro was created at the very end of the twentieth century, all the participating countries signed agreements. They pledged that the creation of the Eurozone was not the creation of a welfare system in which richer countries would transfer wealth to poorer countries. There was also an agreement that participating countries' **budget deficits** would not exceed 3 percent of **gross domestic product (GDP)** in any one country. It took less than a decade for this system to face a series of crises. Some politicians figured out that if they got into trouble, other Eurozone countries would answer their cries for help. After all, no one would want to see the demise of the euro and therefore no one would want to see any Eurozone country collapse and pull out of the one-currency system.

GREECE PAVED THE WAY

Greece has never been a rich country. Apart from its antiquities, Greece has been best known for corruption. For years, the average Greek family has paid about $2,000 annually in "official" bribes. The simple fact is that if you want anything done in Greece, you better grease the skids (no pun intended). Greece was not allowed to join the Eurozone at first, but then was accepted because it showed it had a budget deficit of only 4 percent of GDP. Six months after its acceptance, Greek government officials admitted that the numbers were a little off—its deficit had actually been 12 percent. Eurozone leaders said "tsk, tsk" and asked Greece to behave like a proper member of the one-currency area. After this bit of scolding, Greece disappeared from the financial news headlines.

Then Greece (population: 11.3 million) successfully bid on the 2004 summer Olympics. Conservative estimates place the cost to that small country of at least $15 billion, but the reality is probably much more. Soon after the glow of the XXVIII Olympiad wore off, Greece started having trouble paying its bills. It turned out that government spending was increasing much faster than government revenues. Lenders got nervous, so when Greece went to finance those deficits, its borrowing costs started to rise. It called for help.

THE FIRST GREEK BAILOUT

Help came in the form of "emergency" grants, gifts, and loans from other EU countries in the Eurozone in 2010. Right after the first bailout, seeing how easy it was to get financial help, Greek politicians did not do what they had promised. They sold off no government assets. They reformed no labor laws. They eliminated no corruption. Years later, they are still asking for more time to "fix" their economy and, of course, they are asking for more loans from the rest of their Eurozone partners and from the **International Monetary Fund** (of which the United States is a paying member).

Measured unemployment in Greece is about 25 percent, and among youths about 50 percent. Per-unit labor costs in Greece are higher than they are even in high-wage Germany. But European leaders still think they can "save" Greece with more bailouts.

What we have seen in Greece are the consequences of **moral hazard.** Greek politicians know that they can always get someone else to pay for their mistakes. Hence, they are not so careful and certainly not so reform-minded as to cut government spending and thereby endanger their cushy government jobs that pay high salaries and provide expensive benefits.

Italy—A Larger Greece?

While Italy seems prosperous to many visitors, it, too, has fallen victim to the consequences of moral hazard. As just one example, for years, there was a large group of Italians who could retire from government service in their early 40s. Although this provision has been eliminated for new retirees, there remain half a million former government workers collecting pensions after retiring at an average age of 42.

Italy is also known as one of the European leaders in graft and corruption, some of which is siphoned off by different Mafia organizations. Many government-sponsored and taxpayer-funded public works projects end up unfinished, even decades later. Consider Italy's A3 highway, which was begun in the 1960s. It starts outside of Naples and goes for 300 miles to the south. Today, the A3 is an obstacle course because of construction sites that have lingered for more than twenty years. Some say that organized crime is responsible for the delays. Others say that this situation represents the rotten fruits of a jobs-for-votes culture.

Italy has not asked for a bailout yet, but it may have by the time you read this. Mind you, Italy is not as bad off as the statistics seem to show. It has a thriving **underground economy** that may represent as much as 30 percent of GDP. What is certain is that Italian politicians know that if they do not make the reforms necessary to increase competitiveness and economic growth and to reduce wasteful government spending, other members of the Eurozone will bail them out.

SPAIN, OLÉ!

Italy's neighbor, Spain, claimed for years that it would not need a bailout. The Spanish government's borrowing costs, nonetheless, have stayed high because outside investors are worried that it will not be able to pay back its government debt.

Spain talks big about "austerity." That is the word that few governments want to mention to their electorates, because austerity is supposed to mean reduced government expenditures. In Spain, heeding the wishes of the International Monetary Fund, the **European Central Bank (ECB)**, and Eurozone leaders, the Spanish government declared that it would reduce many expenditures. But at the same time, it promised its citizens a 1 percent increase in pension payments per recipient in 2013. Sound familiar? It is called the don't-kick-me-out-of-office ploy that a politician can make when she or he knows that there is a bailout in the horizon. The ever-present moral hazard problem rears its ugly head again.

Spain's neighbor to the west, Portugal, may be in even worse trouble. Since joining the European Union and the Eurozone, Portuguese labor unions and government workers have succeeded in obtaining much higher salaries. The result is that Portuguese per-unit labor costs are 40 percent higher than those in Germany. Crying on the shoulders of Eurozone leaders, Portuguese politicians have shown how serious they are by not increasing government employee salaries any further. There has been little talk about reducing those bloated salaries.

Portugal, like Spain, has seen its international borrowing costs rise because outside lenders also anticipate the possibility of default on government debt.

I.O.U.s AS FAR AS THE EYE CAN SEE

Adoption of the euro meant that less-developed nations on the periphery of Europe—Greece and Portugal, just to name a few—could borrow as cheaply as core nations, such as France and Germany. Investors in the core nations poured enormous sums into the periphery, much of it spent on new houses, higher pay and pensions for more government employees, and Olympic stadiums. When recession struck in 2007, it became clear that people in Greece, Portugal, and Spain, for example, had borrowed too many euros and would have trouble paying them back.

Let's look at the results: **national debt** per person for the period of 2002–2012 skyrocketed. It increased 142 percent in Portugal, 94 percent in Spain, 90 percent in France, and 105 percent in Greece. The average Greek has a public debt I.O.U. of $39,000. In France that number is $38,000. Spain and Portugal have a per-person public debt of about $24,000.

CALLING THE MONEY LENDERS TO THE RESCUE

Member nations in the Eurozone ceded their monetary independence to the ECB about fifteen years ago. That central bank has a mission similar to that of the Federal Reserve System in the United States—to provide liquidity but never to bailout individual member states. In spite of its charter, the European Central Bank announced in the fall of 2012 that it was embarking on a plan of unlimited buying of the government debt of troubled Eurozone countries. As a consequence, the ECB effectively replaced private credit markets as a cash source for Spain and Italy, thereby lowering their borrowing costs and relieving them of the threat of **insolvency.** And this is so even though the ECB was never supposed to favor countries in crisis over countries that are not facing crises.

Moral hazard is flying around the Eurozone faster than ever. Perhaps for a while, Eurozone citizens will not understand that they are actually subsidizing the profligate ways and lack of labor market reforms in Greece, Italy, Spain, and Portugal.

THE NEW, NEW EUROZONE BAILOUT FUND

The organized bailouts started with the **Interim European Financial Stability Facility.** Then, in 2012 yet another way to provide bailouts was created. It is called the **European Stability Mechanism.** This Eurozone bailout gimmick took two years to design after leaders in the **currency union** had decided to set it up as a permanent safety net for countries in financial troubles. Its charter allows it initially to lend as much as $200 billion euros to governments that are unable to raise funds in international bond markets. By 2014, the fund is supposed to contain $500 billion.

No one quite knows how the new European Stability Mechanism will actually be funded. In principle, all seventeen Eurozone countries must provide the funding based on the size of their economies. In practice, we will offer a prediction: Some of them may just say no thanks. After all, manufacturing activity shrank through 2011 and 2012 in the Eurozone and the EU entered into yet another recession in the fall of 2012. According the World Bank, the European debt crisis will weigh heavily on the world economy for years to come. So where will the seventeen Eurozone members get the money to fill the coffers of the new, bigger and better rescue fund? It surely will not come from weaker countries such as Greece, Italy, Portugal, and Spain.

In any event, all Eurozone countries are jointly liable for the new rescue fund. They are also jointly liable for the ECB's liabilities. No better situation could arise for countries in trouble, such as Greece, Italy, Portugal, and Spain. These nations' governments can keep pretending to tighten their belts, keep pretending to reform their rigid labor markets, and keep pretending that they really are going to have lots of economic growth in the future. They know the truth, though, that their individual liabilities for being bailed out are going to be a small part of the joint liability of all seventeen countries.

WHY CAN'T EUROZONE COUNTRIES POLICE EACH OTHER?

Seeing the disarray in so many Eurozone countries' budgets, member country politicians agreed in the fall of 2012 to form a so-called **fiscal pact**. This Eurozone invention is supposed to involve a central entity that will oversee the budgets of each Eurozone government. Somehow, this oversight mechanism will cause less red ink to flow in each Eurozone country. So far, no procedure has been put in place that would give this new entity the ability to actually force sovereign governments to change their spending and taxing plans.

Oh, and then there is regulation of the banks. Some observers believe that all this talk about debt problems can be laid at the foot of the major banks throughout Europe. First, it is said, they should not have loaned so much prior to the Great Recession. Now, it is said, they are not lending enough after the Great Recession. So, yet another pan-European entity is supposed to regulate all Eurozone banking institutions. Well, the United States has regulators for every type of bank and yet that did not stop the United States from suffering through a near-bank panic and banking meltdown in 2008. Will Europe have any better luck? We predict not.

GREECE, SPAIN, PORTUGAL, AND FRANCE HAVE SOMETHING IN COMMON

When there is talk of austerity, most countries "hunker down." What does this mean in principle and in practice? When Greece revealed its 2013 budget, lo and behold, there were almost no cuts in public spending, no structural reforms, but there were higher taxes. The same occurred in France, Spain, and Portugal.

In France, the fiscal reform bloodletting was to involve one-third decreases in government spending and two-thirds increases in taxes. In reality, public expenditures in France have risen every year for the past 30 years, reaching almost 57 percent of GDP. The chances that such spending will actually be cut are thus low. Spain's proposed budget was a little more evenhanded. About half the reduction in its deficit is supposed to come from lower spending and half from higher taxes. But European citizens have been diligent in evading taxes for a long time. We predict that even though taxes are officially being raised across the Eurozone, most of those new taxes will be evaded. And because government spending is largely resistant to reduction, the crisis will drag on and on. We'll keep you updated.

FOR CRITICAL ANALYSIS

1. Why would a government continue to borrow if it knew it could never pay back all of the loans, including interest?

2. Why would international bond buyers be willing to purchase government bonds from Greece, Spain, Portugal, and Italy when there appears to be some risk that those governments will not be able to pay back those loans? .

3. If labor costs are extremely high in one country compared to another, what is the usual mechanism that allows the high-cost country to still be competitive in its export markets?

4. What are the benefits to the seventeen Eurozone countries of having a common currency? (*Hint*: What are the benefits of the fifty states using dollars, rather than fifty separate monies?)

5. What makes almost all government politicians everywhere in the world continue to spend more than is collected in taxes?

6. What would happen (or is happening!) to Greece if it pulled out of the Eurozone and went back to using its former national currency, the drachma?

CHAPTER 25

The Global Power of the Big Mac

It seems obvious that the average western European or American or Canadian earns a higher income than the average resident of countries such as China and India. What is more difficult to estimate is how *much* better off the citizens are in one nation compared to another. The most obvious obstacle to creating such an estimate is the matter of national currencies. In the United States, for example, we probably want to make income comparisons in dollars. But dollars are not the national currency in Western Europe or in China or India or Japan, so we must somehow convert from one currency to another. How shall we do this?

FOREIGN EXCHANGE RATES

You know that if you take a trip to another country, you will have to pay in the currency of that country. If you go to Europe, in seventeen countries, you will buy goods with euros. If you go to India, you will pay in rupees. If you go to Russia, you will buy using rubles.

So, to compare the average Russian's income in rubles with the average American's income in dollars, we must convert the rubles to the equivalent amount of dollars. The data for converting are readily available on a daily basis. That is because there is a worldwide market in **foreign exchange,** or national currencies. You might find that it takes thirty rubles to buy one dollar. Or you may find that it takes fifty rupees to buy one dollar. So, as a first approximation, this means that to compare incomes across the world, simple arithmetic is involved. We convert, via **foreign exchange rate** tables—found on hundreds of Internet sites—other nations' average incomes in their own currencies to what they are in the U.S. currency, dollars.

For example, if the average income in France is 30,000 euros, we multiply the current euro exchange rate by that number. Suppose that the exchange rate is that one euro equals 1.20 dollars. Then average income in France is 30,000 euros times 1.2 dollars per euro, or $36,000.

When we do such calculations, we find that on an exchange-rate basis, the average American is thirty-five times richer than the average Indian, almost twenty times richer than the average citizen of China, and six times richer than the average Russian.

Problems with Using Market Exchange Rates

Foreign exchange rates are a function of world **supply and demand** (sound familiar?). But demand and supply of currencies is ultimately derived from (or determined by) the demand and supply of, among other things, **traded goods.** Traded goods (and services) are those that, as the name suggest, are traded across national borders. Some examples of traded goods are wines, automobiles, wheat, and shoes. If all goods were traded and if that trade occurred with no distortions, then exchange rates would permit us to perfectly compare incomes around the world.

But there is a complication: Not all goods and services that we consume are traded goods. **Non-traded goods** include houses, haircuts, house-cleaning services, and landscaping, as well as many others. Non-traded goods and service are not involved in exchange across countries' borders.

The existence of non-traded goods implies that bias will result if we use only exchange rates to make international comparison. This is because in poorer countries, wages are low and so non-traded goods (made with that low-cost labor) are likely to be the cheapest. That is, in low-income nations we expect to see restaurant meals, beauty salon services, and house cleaning to be much less expensive than those same items in high-income nations. Hence, if we use current exchange rates—based on traded goods—to convert incomes to a common currency, differences in average incomes between low-wage nations and high-wage nations are going to be exaggerated.

Often, you will read newspaper stories about a developing country in which the average income, say, is $1,000 a year. That number is derived from current foreign exchange rates. It does not take account of how cheaply residents in that country can buy basic foods and services that are not traded in international markets.

Purchasing Power Parity—A Solution?

Somehow we have to adjust current exchange rates to account for differences in the true cost of living across countries. To do so, we may use a concept known as **purchasing power parity,** which creates a type of adjusted foreign exchange rate.[1] The details of how the World Bank and other organizations calculate various purchasing power parity measures for 180 countries are not important here. Suffice it to say that, in doing so, attempts are made to correct market foreign exchange rates for the relative cost of living in each country. So, on a purchasing power parity basis—taking into account the lower cost of living in India, China, and Russia—average income in the United States is only thirteen times higher than in India, eight and a half times higher than in China, and a little over three times higher than in Russia.

A major problem remains, nonetheless. Purchasing power adjustments are difficult to calculate in each country. The residents of each nation buy different combinations of goods and services or, in the alternative, they buy similar goods and services but with subtle variations in quality. Not only are the calculations difficult. There are disputes over the best way to do them for each country, leading to doubts about whether the measures *really* account for differences in the cost of living.

It is here that a humble sandwich enters our story.

BIG MAC TO THE RESCUE

Since 1967, a monster burger called the Big Mac has been a featured item on the menu of McDonalds restaurants. A typical Big Mac is created using virtually identical ingredients around the world (although substitution occurs where religious or cultural norms rule out beef). Big Macs are produced according to a uniform process detailed in the McDonalds 600-page manual. As well as being a "standard product," local prices of Big Macs are not distorted by international transportation and distribution costs.

In light of these facts, since 1986, the magazine *The Economist* has developed a Big Mac Index. By using one good only—a Big Mac—*The Economist* has thereby created a means of comparing the cost of living around the world, and also a means of determining how much exchange rates fail to account for non-traded goods.

Keeping in mind that the methods of production and the ingredients are the same in Big Macs everywhere, if we convert international Big Mac prices using exchange rates, we "should" get exactly the same price everywhere. But if, using exchange rates, we calculate that a Big Mac costs $6.80 in Switzerland, but only $4.20 in the United States, this says that a dollar does not go very far in Switzerland. That is, the cost of living in Switzerland is relatively high, most likely because non-traded goods (such as housing) are quite expensive there. Similarly, if we also find that, at current exchange rates, a Big Mac costs the equivalent of $2.40 in China, we have found that

---

1 Obviously, there is no market for anything measured in units of purchasing power parity.

the dollar goes a long way there: The cost of living is low in China compared to that in the United States. Again, this is most likely because non-traded goods made with low-wage labor are quite cheap in China. The upshot is that if we adjust incomes using the Big Mac index to correct for differences in the cost of living, we can get a much better idea of relative real incomes. In one recent year, for example, using exchange rates, income in Switzerland was about $83,000, compared to about $48,000 in the United States. After correcting with the aid of the Big Mac, however, we find that real income in Switzerland is only about $52,000—still higher than that in the United States, but not by much.

McWages, Real Wages, and Well-Being

Now consider creating a McWage. Given that the talent necessary to make a Big Mac is about the same everywhere, we can collect information on the wages of Big Mac preparers throughout the world. This will provide us with a comparison of the cost of hiring that uniform quality of labor across countries. If we then take McWages and divide them by the local price of a Big Mac, we can discern how many Big Mac equivalents each worker is paid per hour. This is a simple, albeit one-good specific, measure of the **real wage,** that is, the wage rate adjusted for the cost of living in each nation. And this measure—"Big Macs per hour"—can be constructed without worrying about biases in exchange rates or complicated purchasing power parity calculations.

That is exactly what economists Orley Ashenfelter and Stepan Jurajda have done. They have found that workers in the United States earn about 2.5 Big Macs per hour (or BMPH), compared to the 3.1 BMPH earned in Japan. In Canada, and Western Europe, workers are paid about 2.2 BMPH. Using the same calculations, the authors find that workers in Russia earn about 1.2 BMPH, while Eastern European workers collect about 0.8. Workers in China earn about 0.6 BMPH, while those in India earn only about 0.4. The bottom line is that using the BMPH index, we see that standards of living vary greatly around the world, but not nearly to the extent that is suggested by exchange rates.

Trends in Productivity

A basic tenet of economics is that in competitive labor markets (and that is certainly where McDonalds gets its workers) people are paid based on what they produce. Thus, using the data mentioned above, we can infer that workers in the United States are only about 10 percent more productive than those in Canada or Western Europe, but they are about four times as productive as those in China.

We can also look at the patterns of change in the BMPH index over time, to give us an idea of how **productivity**, and thus the standard of living, is evolving around the world. As one example, between 2000 and 2007, McWages in the United States rose by 13 percent while the price of a Big Mac jumped by 21 percent. That means that real wages *fell* in the United States by about 8 percent over this period. By the same calculation for the same period, productivity and thus real wages rose 60 percent in China and by over 50 percent in India. Clearly, average productivity was rising sharply in these two countries.

During 2007–2011, the most recent period for which complete data are available, real wages have fallen even more in developed nations such as the United States, Canada, and Western Europe. In most developing nations, real wages have been rising, although much more slowly than before. The good news of this story is thus that developing nations are generally closing the standard of living gap. The bad news is that the world financial crisis and its aftermath have diminished opportunities around the world, a development that is surely worth monitoring in the future.

For Critical Analysis

1. Assume you are going to take a trip to Paris. You buy euros at your local bank or at the airport. Then you start spending them once you are in Paris. Every time you buy something there, you explicitly or implicitly translate the euro price into dollars. Often, you might say to yourself, "how do Parisians afford such high prices?" What is wrong with this line of reasoning? (*Hint:* In what currency do Parisians earn their income?)

2. Why don't the local prices of restaurant meals, haircuts, and gardening services affect a country's exchange rate?

3. If the same amount of materials and the same methods are used to produce Big Macs in over 120 countries, why are the prices of Big Macs not all the same, expressed in dollars?

4. Is there anything that a Big Mac preparer in a developing country can do to earn a higher real wage rate?

5. Why does McDonalds provide a 600-page manual to the company's franchises in every country? (*Hint:* What are the ways that any franchisor can monitor quality of its franchisees?)

6. In a wealthy country, wages are high not only in the traded goods and services sector but also in the non-traded goods and services sector. Why? (*Hint:* Are there two separate labor markets or just one?)

CHAPTER **26**

The Opposition to Globalization

The last twenty years has been a time of great change on the international trade front. The North American Free Trade Agreement (NAFTA), for example, substantially reduced **trade barriers** among citizens of Canada, the United States, and Mexico. On a global scale, the Uruguay Round of the General Agreement on Tariffs and Trade (GATT) was ratified by 117 nations including the United States. Under the terms of this agreement, the **World Trade Organization (WTO),** whose membership now numbers more than 150, replaced GATT, and **tariffs** were cut worldwide. Agricultural **subsidies** were also reduced, and patent protections were extended. The WTO has also established arbitration boards to settle international disputes over trade issues.

THE GAINS FROM TRADE

Many economists believe that both NAFTA and the agreements reached during the Uruguay Round were victories not only for free trade and **globalization** (the integration of national economies into an international economy) but also for the citizens of the participating nations. Nevertheless, many noneconomists, particularly politicians, opposed these agreements, so it is important to understand what is beneficial about NAFTA, the Uruguay Round, the WTO, and free trade and globalization.

Voluntary trade creates new **wealth.** In voluntary trade, both parties in an exchange gain. They give up something of lesser value to them in return for something of greater value to them. In this sense, exchanges are always unequal. But it is this unequal nature of exchange that is the source of the increased **productivity** and higher wealth that occur whenever trade takes place. When we engage in exchange, what we give up is worth less than what we get—if this were not true, we would not have traded. What is true for us is also true for our trading partner, meaning that the partner is better off, too. (Of course, sometimes after an exchange, you may believe that you were mistaken about the value of what you just received—this is called *buyer's remorse*, but it does not affect our discussion.)

Free trade encourages individuals to employ their abilities in the most productive manner possible and to exchange the fruits of their efforts. The **gains from trade** arise from one of the fundamental ideas in economics: A nation gains from doing what it can do best *relative to other nations*, that is, by specializing in those endeavors in which it has a **comparative advantage.** Trade encourages individuals and nations to discover ways to specialize so that they can become more productive and enjoy higher incomes. Increased productivity and the subsequent increase in the rate of **economic growth** are exactly what the signatories of the Uruguay Round and NAFTA sought—and are obtaining—by reducing trade barriers and thus increasing globalization.

KEEPING THE COMPETITION OUT

Despite the enormous gains from exchange, some people (sometimes a great many of them) routinely oppose free trade, particularly in the case of international trade. This opposition comes in many guises, but they all basically come down to one: When our borders are open to trade with other nations, this exposes some individuals and businesses in our nation to more **competition.** Most firms and workers hate competition, and who can blame them? After all, if a firm can keep competitors out, its **profits** are sure to stay the same or even rise. Also, if workers can prevent competition from other sources, they can enjoy higher wages and perhaps a larger selection of jobs. So the real source of most opposition to globalization is that the opponents of trade dislike the competition that comes with it. This position is not immoral or unethical, but it is not altruistic or noble, either. It is based on self-interest, pure and simple.

Opposition to globalization is nothing new, by the way. In the twentieth century, it culminated most famously in the Smoot–Hawley Tariff Act of 1930. This federal statute was a classic example of **protectionism**—an effort to protect a subset of U.S. producers at the expense of consumers and other producers. It included tariff schedules for over 20,000 products, raising taxes on affected imports by an average of 52 percent.

The Smoot–Hawley Tariff Act encouraged so-called *beggar-thy-neighbor* policies by the rest of the world. Such policies are an attempt to improve (a portion of) one's domestic economy at the expense of foreign countries' economies. In this case, tariffs were imposed to discourage imports in the hope that domestic import-competing industries would benefit. France, the Netherlands, Switzerland, and the United Kingdom soon adopted beggar-thy-neighbor policies to counter the American ones. The result was a massive reduction in international trade. According to many economists, this caused a worldwide worsening of the Great Depression.

Opponents of globalization sometimes claim that beggar-thy-neighbor policies really do benefit the United States by protecting import-competing industries. In general, this claim is not correct. It is true that *some* Americans benefit from such policies, but two large groups of Americans lose. First, the purchasers of imports and import-competing goods suffer from the higher prices and reduced selection of goods and suppliers caused by tariffs and import **quotas.** Second, the decline in imports caused by protectionism also causes a decline in *exports*, thereby harming firms and workers in these industries.

This result follows directly from one of the fundamental propositions in international trade: *In the long run, imports are paid for by exports.* This proposition simply states that when one country buys goods and services from the rest of the world (imports), the rest of the world eventually wants goods from that country (exports) in exchange. Given this fundamental proposition, a corollary becomes obvious: *Any restriction on imports leads to a reduction in exports.* Thus, any extra business for import-competing industries gained as a result of tariffs or quotas means at least as much business *lost* for exporting industries.

The Arguments against Globalization

Opponents of globalization often raise a variety of objections in their efforts to reduce it. For example, it is sometimes claimed that foreign companies engage in **dumping,** which is selling their goods in the United States "below cost." The first question to ask when such charges are made is, below *whose* cost? Clearly, if the foreign firm is selling in the United States, it must be offering the good for sale at a price that is at or below the costs of U.S. firms. Otherwise it could not induce Americans to buy it. But the ability of individuals or firms to obtain goods at lower cost is one of the *benefits* of free trade, not one of its harmful aspects.

What about claims that import sales are taking place at prices below the foreign company's costs? This amounts to arguing that the owners of the foreign company are voluntarily giving some of their wealth to us, namely, the difference between their costs and the (lower) price they charge us. It is possible, though unlikely, that they might wish to do this, perhaps because this could be the cheapest way of getting us to try a product that we would not otherwise purchase. But even supposing it is true, why would we want to refuse this gift? As a nation, we are richer if we accept it. Moreover, it is a gift that will be offered for only a short time. There is no point in selling at prices below cost unless the seller hopes to soon raise the price profitably above cost!

Another argument sometimes raised against globalization is that the goods are produced abroad using "unfair" labor practices (such as the use of child labor) or production processes that do not meet U.S. environmental standards. Such charges are sometimes true. But we must remember two things here. First, although we may find the use of child labor (or perhaps sixty-hour workweeks with no overtime pay) objectionable, such practices were at one time commonplace in the United States. They were common here for the same reason they are currently practiced abroad. The people involved were (or are) too poor to do otherwise. Some families in developing nations cannot survive unless all family members contribute. As unfortunate as this situation is, if we insist on imposing our values and attitudes—shaped in part by our high wealth—on peoples whose wealth is far lower than ours, we run the risk of making them worse off even as we think we are helping them.

Similar considerations apply to environmental standards.[1] Individuals' and nations' willingness to pay for environmental quality is very much shaped by their wealth. Environmental quality is a **normal good.** This means that people who are rich (such as Americans) want to consume more of it per capita than people who are poor. Insisting that other nations meet environmental standards that we find acceptable is much like insisting that they wear the clothes we wear, use the modes of transportation we prefer, and consume the foods we like. The few people who can afford it will indeed be living in the style to which we are accustomed, but most people in developing countries will not be able to afford anything like that style.

Our point is not that foreign labor or environmental standards are, or should be, irrelevant to Americans. Instead, our point is that achieving high standards of either is costly, and trade restrictions are unlikely to be the most efficient or effective way to achieve them. Just as important, labor standards and environmental standards are all too often raised as smokescreens to hide the real motive: keeping the competition out.

---

1 There is one important exception to this statement. When foreign air or water pollution is generated near enough to our borders (e.g., in Mexico or Canada) to cause harm to Americans, good public policy presumably dictates that we seek to treat that pollution as though it were being generated inside our borders.

WHY ARE ANTITRADE MEASURES PASSED?

If globalization is beneficial and restrictions on trade are generally harmful, how does legislation such as the Smoot–Hawley Tariff Act and other restrictions on international trade ever get passed? The explanation is that because foreign competition often affects a narrow and specific import-competing industry, such as textiles, shoes, or automobiles, trade restrictions are crafted to benefit a narrow, well-defined group of economic agents. For example, limits on imports of Japanese automobiles in the 1980s chiefly benefited workers and owners of the Big Three automakers in this country: General Motors, Ford, and Chrysler. Similarly, long-standing quotas that limit imports of sugar benefit the owners of a handful of large U.S. sugar producers. Because of the concentrated benefits that accrue when Congress votes in favor of trade restrictions, sufficient funds can be raised in those industries to aggressively lobby members of Congress to impose those restrictions.

The eventual reduction in exports that must follow is normally spread throughout all export industries. Consequently, no specific group of workers, managers, or shareholders in export industries will be motivated to contribute funds to lobby Congress to reduce international trade restrictions. Further, although consumers of imports and import-competing goods lose due to trade restrictions, they, too, are typically a diffuse group of individuals, none of whom will be greatly affected individually by any particular import restriction. This simultaneous existence of concentrated benefits and diffuse costs led Mark Twain to observe long ago that the free traders win the arguments but the **protectionists** win the votes.

Of course, the protectionists don't win *all* the votes—after all, about one-seventh of the U.S. economy is based on international trade. Despite the opposition to free trade that comes from many quarters, its benefits to the economy as a whole are so great that it is unthinkable that we might do away with international trade altogether. Both economic theory and empirical evidence clearly indicate that on balance, Americans are better off with freer trade achieved through such developments as NAFTA and the WTO.

FOR CRITICAL ANALYSIS

1. For a number of years, Japanese automakers voluntarily limited the number of cars they exported to the United States. What effect do you think this had on Japanese imports of U.S. cars and U.S. exports of goods and services *other than* automobiles?

2. Until a few years ago, U.S. cars exported to Japan had the driver controls on the left side (as in the United States). The Japanese (like the British), however, drive on the left side of the road, so Japanese cars sold in Japan have the driver controls on the right side. Suppose the Japanese tried to sell their cars in the United States with the driver controls on the right side. What impact would this likely have on their sales in this country? Do you think the unwillingness of U.S. carmakers to put the driver controls on the "correct" side for exports to Japan had any effect on their sales of cars in that country?

3. Keeping in mind the key propositions of globalization outlined in this chapter, what is the likely impact of international trade restrictions on the following variables in the United States: employment, the unemployment rate, real GDP, and the price level? Explain your responses.

4. During the late 1980s and early 1990s, American automobile manufacturers greatly increased the quality of the cars they produced relative to the quality of the cars produced in other nations. What effect do you think this had on American imports of Japanese cars, Japanese imports of American cars, and American exports of goods and services other than automobiles?

5. The U.S. government subsidizes the export of U.S.-manufactured commercial aircraft. What effect do you think this policy has on American imports of foreign goods and American exports of products other than commercial aircraft? Explain.

6. Who bears the costs and enjoys the benefits of the subsidies mentioned in the previous question?

CHAPTER **27**

The $750,000 Job

In even-numbered years, particularly years evenly divisible by four, politicians of all persuasions are apt to give long-winded speeches about the need to protect U.S. jobs from the evils of **globalization.** To accomplish this goal, we are encouraged to "buy American." If further encouragement is needed, we are told that if we do not voluntarily reduce the amount of imported goods we purchase, the government will impose (or make more onerous) **tariffs** (taxes) on imported goods or **quotas** (quantity restrictions) that physically limit imports. The objective of this exercise is to "save U.S. jobs."

Unlike black rhinos or blue whales, U.S. jobs are in no danger of becoming extinct. There are virtually an unlimited number of potential jobs in the U.S. economy, and there always will be. Some of these jobs are not very pleasant, and many others do not pay very well, but there will always be employment of some sort as long as there is **scarcity.** Thus when steelworkers making $72,000 per year say that imports of foreign steel should be reduced to save their jobs, what they really mean is this: They want to be protected from **competition** so that they can continue their present employment at the same or a higher salary rather than move to different jobs that have less desirable working conditions or pay less. There is nothing wrong with the steelworkers' goal (better working conditions and higher pay), but it has nothing to do with "saving jobs."

THE GAINS FROM GLOBALIZATION

In any discussion of the consequences of international trade restrictions, it is essential to remember two facts. First, *we pay for imports with exports.* It is true that in the short run, we can sell off **assets** or borrow from abroad if we happen to import more goods and services than we export. But we have only a finite amount of assets to sell, and foreigners will not wait forever for us to pay our bills. Ultimately, our accounts can be settled only if we provide (export) goods and services to the trading partners from whom we purchase (import) goods and services. Trade, after all, involves a *quid pro quo* (literally, "something for something").

The second point to remember is that *voluntary trade is mutually beneficial to the trading partners.* If we restrict international trade, we reduce those benefits, both for our trading partners and for ourselves. One way these reduced benefits are manifested is in the form of curtailed employment opportunities for workers. The reasoning is simple. Other countries will buy our goods only if they can market theirs because they, too, have to export goods to pay for their imports. Thus, any U.S. restrictions on imports to this country—via tariffs, quotas, or other means—ultimately cause a reduction in our exports because other countries will be unable to pay for our goods. This implies that import restrictions must inevitably decrease the size of our export sector. Thus, imposing trade restrictions to save jobs in import-competing industries has the effect of costing jobs in export industries. Most studies have shown that the net effect seems to be reduced employment overall.

THE ADVERSE EFFECTS OF TRADE RESTRICTIONS

Import restrictions also impose costs on U.S. consumers as a whole. By reducing competition from abroad, quotas, tariffs, and other trade restraints push up the prices of foreign goods and enable U.S. producers to hike their own prices. Perhaps the best-documented example of this effect is found in the automobile industry, where "voluntary" restrictions on Japanese imports were in place for more than a decade.

Due in part to the enhanced quality of imported cars, sales of domestically produced automobiles fell from 9 million units in 1978 to an average of 6 million units per year between 1980 and 1982. Profits of U.S. automakers plummeted as well, and some incurred substantial losses. The automobile manufacturers' and autoworkers' unions demanded protection from import competition. Politicians from automobile-producing states rallied to their cause. The result was a "voluntary" agreement by Japanese car companies (the most important competitors of U.S. firms) to restrict their U.S. sales to 1.68 million units per year. This agreement—which amounted to a quota, even though it never officially bore that name—began in April 1981 and continued well into the 1990s in various forms.

Robert W. Crandall, an economist with the Brookings Institution, estimated how much this voluntary trade restriction cost U.S. consumers in higher car prices. According to his estimates, the reduced supply of Japanese cars pushed their prices up by $2,000 per car, measured in 2013 dollars. The higher prices of Japanese imports in turn enabled domestic producers to hike their prices an average of $800 per car. The total tab in the first full year of the program was over $8 billion. Crandall also estimated that about 26,000 jobs in automobile-related industries were protected by the voluntary import restrictions. Dividing $8 billion by 26,000 jobs yields a cost to consumers of more than $300,000 *per year* for every job preserved in the automobile industry. U.S. consumers could have saved nearly $5 billion on their car purchases each year if instead of implicitly agreeing to import restrictions, they had simply given $100,000 in cash to every autoworker whose job was protected by the voluntary import restraints.

The same types of calculations have been made for other industries. Tariffs in the apparel industry were increased between 1977 and 1981, preserving the jobs of about 116,000 U.S. apparel workers at a cost of $45,000 per job each year. The cost of **protectionism** has been even higher in other industries. Jobs preserved in the glassware industry due to trade restrictions cost $200,000 apiece each year. In the maritime industry, the yearly cost of trade restriction is $290,000 per job. In the steel industry, the cost of protecting a job has been estimated at an astounding $750,000 per year. If free trade were permitted, each steelworker losing a job could be given a cash payment of half that amount each year, and consumers would still save a lot of **wealth.**

The Real Impact on Jobs

What is more, none of these cost studies has attempted to estimate the ultimate impact of import restrictions on the flow of exports, the number of workers who lose their jobs in the export sector, and thus total employment in the economy.

Remember that imports pay for exports and that our imports are the exports of our trading partners. So when imports to the United States are restricted, our trading partners will necessarily buy less of what *we* produce. The resulting decline in export sales means less employment in exporting industries. And the total reduction in trade leads to less employment for workers such as stevedores (who load and unload ships) and truck drivers (who carry goods to and from ports). On both counts—the overall cut in trade and the accompanying fall in exports—protectionism leads to employment declines that might not be obvious immediately.

Some years ago, Congress tried to pass a "domestic-content" bill for automobiles. The legislation would have required that cars sold in the

United States have a minimum percentage of their components manufactured and assembled in this country. Proponents of the legislation argued that it would have protected 300,000 jobs in the U.S. automobile manufacturing and auto parts supply industries. Yet the legislation's supporters failed to recognize the negative impact of the bill on trade in general and its ultimate impact on U.S. export industries. A U.S. Department of Labor study did recognize these impacts, estimating that the domestic-content legislation would have cost more jobs in trade-related and export industries than it protected in import-competing businesses. Congress ultimately decided not to impose a domestic-content requirement for cars sold in the United States.

THE LONG-RUN FAILURE OF IMPORT CONTROLS

In principle, trade restrictions are imposed to provide economic help to specific industries and to increase employment in those industries. Ironically, the long-term effects may be just the opposite. Researchers at the **World Trade Organization (WTO)** examined employment in three industries that have been heavily protected throughout the world: textiles, clothing, and iron and steel. Despite stringent **protectionist** measures, employment in these industries actually declined during the period of protection, sometimes dramatically. In textiles, employment fell 22 percent in the United States and 46 percent in the European Common Market (the predecessor of the **European Union**). Employment losses in the clothing industry ranged from 18 percent in the United States to 56 percent in Sweden. Losses in the iron and steel industry ranged from 10 percent in Canada to 54 percent in the United States. In short, the WTO researchers found that restrictions on free trade were no guarantee against employment losses, even in the industries supposedly being protected.

The evidence seems clear: The cost of protecting jobs in the short run is enormous, and in the long run it appears that jobs cannot be protected, especially if one considers all aspects of protectionism. Free trade is a tough platform on which to run for office, but it is likely to be the one that will yield the most general benefits if implemented. Of course, this does not mean that politicians will embrace it. So we end up "saving jobs" at an annual cost of $750,000 each.

FOR CRITICAL ANALYSIS

1. If it would be cheaper to give each steelworker $375,000 per year in cash than impose restrictions on steel imports, why do we have the import restrictions rather than the cash payments?

2. Most U.S. imports and exports travel through our seaports at some point. How do you predict that members of Congress from coastal states would vote on proposals to restrict international trade? What other information would you want to know in making such a prediction?

3. Who gains and who loses from import restrictions? In answering, you should consider both consumers and producers in both the country that imposes the restrictions and in the other countries affected by them. Also, be sure to take into account the effects of import restrictions on *export* industries.

4. When you go shopping for a new computer, is your real objective to "import" a computer into your apartment, or is it to "export" cash from your wallet? What does this tell you about the true object of international trade—is it imports or exports?

5. Some U.S. policy is designed to subsidize exports and thus increase employment in export industries. What effect does such policy have on our imports of foreign goods and thus on employment in industries that compete with imports?

6. What motivates politicians to impose trade restrictions?

Glossary

abject poverty: surviving on the equivalent of $1 or less of income per person per day

adverse selection: a process in which "undesirable" (high-cost or high-risk) participants tend to dominate one side of a market, causing adverse effects for the other side; often results from asymmetric information

aggregate demand: the total value of all planned spending on goods and services by all economic entities in the economy

appropriations bills: legislation that determines the size of government discretionary spending

asset: any valuable good capable of yielding flows of income or services over time

asset-backed security (ABS): a bond that has other assets (such as home mortgages) as collateral

asymmetric information: a circumstance in which participants on one side of a market have more information than those on the other side of the market; often results in adverse selection

average tax rate: total taxes divided by income

balance sheet: a written record of assets and liabilities

bank run: an attempt by many of a bank's depositors to convert checkable and savings deposits into currency because of a perceived fear for the bank's solvency

bankruptcy: a state of being legally declared unable to pay one's debts so that some or all of the indebtedness is legally wiped out by the courts

Bankruptcy Code: the set of federal laws and regulations governing the process of declaring bankruptcy

bond: a debt conferring the right to receive a specific series of money payments in the future

bondholders: the owners of government or corporate bonds

book value: asset valuations that are based on the original purchase price of the assets rather than current market values

budget constraint: all of the possible combinations of goods that can be purchased at given prices and given income

budget deficit: the excess of government spending over government revenues during a given time period

business cycles: the ups and downs in overall business activity, evidenced by changes in GDP, employment, and the price level

capital stock: the collection of productive assets that can be combined with other inputs, such as labor, to produce goods and services

cash and non-cash transfers: payments and services provided by the government to individuals deemed worthy of their receipt

cash flow: cash receipts minus cash payments

central bank: a banker's bank, usually a government institution that also serves as the country's treasury's bank; central banks normally regulate commercial banks

checkable deposits: accounts at depository institutions that are payable on demand, either by means of a check or by direct withdrawal, as through an automated teller machine (ATM)

civil law system: a legal system in which statutes passed by legislatures and executive decrees, rather than judicial decisions based on precedent, form the basis for most legal rules

collateral: assets that are forfeited in the event of default on an obligation

commercial bank: a financial institution that accepts demand deposits, makes loans, and provides other financial services to the public

common law system: a legal system in which judicial decisions based on precedent, rather than executive decrees or statutes passed by legislatures, form the basis for most legal rules

comparative advantage: the ability to produce a good or service at a lower opportunity cost compared to other producers

constant-quality price: price adjusted for any change in the quality of the good or service

consumer price index (CPI): a measure of the dollar cost of purchasing a bundle of goods and services assumed to be representative of the consumption pattern of a typical consumer; one measure of the price level

consumption: spending by consumers on new goods and services

core inflation: a measure of the overall rate of change in prices of goods, excluding energy and food

cost of living: the dollar cost (relative to a base year) of achieving a given level of satisfaction

creative destruction: the ultimate outcome of a competitive process in which innovation continually creates new products and firms and replaces existing firms and products

creditor: an institution or individual that is owed money by another institution or individual

currency: paper money and coins issued by the government to serve as a medium of exchange

currency union: an agreement among independent governments to use a common medium of exchange

default: failure to meet obligations, for example, the failure to make debt payments

default risk: an estimation combining the probability that a contract will not be adhered to and the magnitude of the loss that will occur if it is not

deficit: excess of government spending over tax receipts during a given fiscal year

deflation: a decline in the average level of the prices of goods and services

deindustrialization: a process of social and economic change caused by the removal or reduction of industrial capacity or activity in a country or region

demand: the willingness and ability to purchase goods

depository institutions: financial institutions that accept deposits from savers and lend those deposits out to borrowers

depression: a severe recession

direct foreign investment: resources provided to individuals and firms in a nation by individuals or firms located in other countries, often taking the form of foreign subsidiary or branch operations of a parent company

disability payments: cash payments made to persons whose physical or mental disabilities prevent them from working

discouraged workers: persons who have dropped out of the labor force because they are unable to find suitable work

discretionary spending: government spending that is decided on anew each year, rather than being determined by a formula or set of rules

disposable income: income remaining after all taxes, retirement contributions, and the like are deducted

dividends: payments made by a corporation to owners of shares of its stock, generally based on the corporation's profits

dumping: the sale of goods in a foreign country at a price below the market price charged for the same goods in the domestic market or at a price below the cost of production

dynamic economic analysis: a mode of analysis that recognizes that people respond to changes in incentives and that takes these responses into account when evaluating the effects of policies

Earned Income Tax Credit: a federal tax program that permits negative taxes, that is, that provides for payments to people (instead of collecting taxes from them) if their incomes go below a predetermined level

economic growth: sustained increases in real per capita income

economic safety net: the set of government programs (such as unemployment insurance and food stamps) that people can call upon when their incomes are low

economies of scale: reductions in average costs achieved by expanding the scale of operations

elasticity: a measure of the responsiveness of one variable to a change in another variable

entitlement programs: government programs for which spending is determined chiefly by formulas or rules that specify who is eligible for funds and how much they may receive

equity: assets minus liabilities; net asset value

European Central Bank (ECB): the central bank for the group of nations that use the euro as their monetary unit

European Stability Mechanism: a 2012 agreement among users of the euro that provides for international guarantees and transfers, for the purpose of preventing default among nations using the euro

European Union (EU): a supranational entity resulting from an agreement among European nations to closely integrate the economic, political, and legal systems of the twenty-seven individual member nations

e-wallet: software that enables users to make electronic commerce transactions securely and quickly

excess reserves: funds kept on hand by commercial banks to meet the transactions demands of customers and to serve as precautionary sources of funds in the event of a bank run; may be held as vault cash or as deposits at the Fed

excess supply: an excess of the quantity supplied of a good over the quantity demanded, evaluated at a given relative price for the good

exchange rate: the price of a currency expressed in terms of another currency

expansion: a period in which economic activity, measured by industrial production, employment, real income, and wholesale and retail sales, is growing on a sustained basis

expansive monetary policy: actions that tend to increase the level or rate of growth of the money supply

expected rate of inflation: the rate at which the average level of prices of goods and services is expected to rise

face value: the denomination in terms of a unit of account expressed on a coin or unit of currency

Fannie Mae: U.S. government–sponsored enterprise established in 1938 to facilitate the market in home mortgages

federal budget deficit: the excess of the national government's spending over its receipts

federal funds rate: the nominal interest rate at which banks can borrow reserves from one another

Federal Reserve System (the Fed): the central bank of the United States

fiscal pact: an agreement among independent governments to jointly monitor the spending and taxing of the nations that are part of the agreement

fiscal policy: discretionary changes in government spending or taxes that alter the overall state of the economy, including employment, investment, and output

fiscal year: the accounting year used by a government or business; for the federal government, the fiscal year runs from October 1 to September 30

flexible exchange rates: exchange rates that are free to move in response to market forces

foreclosure: the legal process by which a borrower in default under a mortgage is deprived of his or her interest in the mortgaged property

foreign exchange: national currencies

foreign exchange rate: the relative price between two national currencies

Freddie Mac: U.S. government–sponsored enterprise established in 1970 to facilitate the market in home mortgages

fully funded pension liability: an obligation to make postretirement contractual payment made to an individual that is guaranteed by a sufficient amount of assets as to make the payment virtually certain

gains from trade: the extent to which individuals, firms, or nations benefit from engaging in voluntary exchange

globalization: the integration of national economies into an international economy

government-sponsored enterprise (GSE): a federally chartered corporation that is privately owned, designed to provide a source of credit nationwide, and limited to servicing one economic sector

gross domestic product (GDP): the dollar value of all new, domestically produced final goods and services in an economy

gross public debt: all public debt, including that owned by agencies of the government issuing it

hedge funds: investment companies that require large initial deposits by investors and pursue high-risk investments in the hope of achieving high returns

human capital: the productive capacity of human beings

illiquid: when used in reference to a company or person—having insufficient cash on hand to meet current liabilities; when used in reference to an asset—that which cannot be easily and cheaply converted into cash

in-kind transfer: the provision of goods and services rather than cash, as in the case of Medicare, Medicaid, or subsidized housing

incentives: positive or negatives consequences of actions

income mobility: the tendency of people to move around in the income distribution over time

industrial policy: a set of government actions that attempt to influence which firms succeed and which fail

Industrial Revolution: the widespread radical socioeconomic changes that took place in England and many other nations beginning in the late eighteenth century brought about when extensive mechanization of production systems resulted in a shift from home-based hand manufacturing to large-scale factory production

inefficient: an outcome that fails to maximize the value of a resource

inflation: a rise in the average level of the prices of goods and services

inflation tax: the decline in the real value or purchasing power of money balances due to inflation

inflationary premium: the additional premium, in percent per year, that people are willing to pay to have dollars sooner rather than later simply because inflation is expected in the future

inside information: valuable information about future economic performance that is not generally available to the public

insolvent: describing a financial condition in which the value of one's assets is less than that of one's liabilities

insourcing: the use of domestic workers to perform a service traditionally done by foreign workers

institutions: the basic rules, customs, and practices of society

interagency borrowings: loans from one part of the federal government to another

interest group: a collection of individuals with common aims

Interim European Financial Stability Facility: a temporary agreement among users of the euro that provides for international guarantees and transfers, for the purpose of preventing default among nations using the euro; succeeded in 2012 by the European Stability Mechanism

intermediate goods: goods that contribute to present or future consumer welfare but are not direct sources of utility themselves; typically, they are used up in the production of final goods and services

International Monetary Fund: an international association of nations created in 1945 to promote international trade and stability of exchange rates

investment: the creation of new machines, factories, and other assets that enable the production of more goods and services in the future

investment bank: a financial institution that helps companies or municipalities obtain financing by selling stocks or bonds on their behalf

labor force: individuals aged 16 and over who either have jobs or are looking and available for work

labor supply curve: a schedule showing the quantity of labor supplied at each wage rate

legal tender: coins or paper money that must be accepted if offered in payment

liabilities: amounts owed; the legal claims against an individual or against an institution by those who are not owners of that institution

loophole: a provision of the tax code that enables a narrow group of beneficiaries to achieve a lower effective tax rate

lump sum tax rebates: fixed cash payments made by a government to taxpayers that are independent of taxpayer income

mandates: in the context of governments, regulations or laws that require other governments, private individuals, or firms to spend money to achieve goals specified by the government

margin: increment or decrement

marginal tax rate: the percentage of the last dollar earned that is paid in taxes

median age: the age that separates the older half of the population from the younger half

median income: the income that separates the higher-income half of the population from the lower-income half

Medicaid: joint federal-state health insurance program for low-income individuals

Medicare: federal health insurance program for individuals aged 65 and above

medium of exchange: any asset that sellers will generally accept as payment

mercantilists—believers in the doctrine of mercantilism, which asserted (among other things) that exports were the principal objective of international trade because they permitted the accumulation of gold

microeconomics: the study of decision making by consumers and by firms and of the market equilibria that result

monetary policy: the use of changes in the amount of money in circulation to affect interest rates, credit markets, inflation (or deflation), and unemployment

money supply: the sum of checkable deposits and currency in the hands of the public

moral hazard: the tendency of an entity insulated from risk to behave differently than it would behave if it were fully exposed to the risk

mortgage-backed security (MBS): a debt obligation that pledges home mortgages as collateral

mortgages: debts that are incurred to buy a house and provide that if the debt is not paid, the house can be sold by the creditor and the proceeds used to pay that debt

mutual funds: a pools of money that are invested in assets, often shares of stock in corporations

national debt: cumulative excess of federal spending over federal tax collections over time; total explicit indebtedness of the federal government

natural resource endowments: the collection of naturally occurring minerals (such as oil and iron ore) and living things (such as forests and fish stocks) that can be used to produce goods and services

near-field communication (NFC): the technology that enables radio communication between smartphones and other devices that are close by, without actually touching the device

negative tax: a payment from the government to an individual that is based on that individual's income

net public debt: the portion of the public debt that is owned outside of the government issuing it

net worth: the excess of assets over liabilities

nominal: an amount expressed in terms of a nation's unit of account

nominal income: income expressed in terms of a monetary unit, such as the dollar

nominal interest rate: the premium, in percent per year, that people are willing to pay to have dollars sooner rather than later

nominal prices: the exchange value of goods, expressed in terms of a unit of account, such as the dollar or the euro

non-traded goods: goods and services not exchanged across international borders

normal good: a good for which the demand increases as people's income or wealth grows

open market: the market for U.S. Treasury securities

opportunity cost: the highest-valued, next-best alternative that must be sacrificed to obtain something

outsourcing: the use of labor in another country to perform service work traditionally done by domestic workers

pay-as-you-go system: a scheme in which current cash outflows are funded (paid for) with current cash inflows

payments system: the institutional infrastructure that enables payments for goods and services to be made

payroll taxes: taxes that are levied on income specifically generated by workforce participation and that are generally earmarked for spending on specific programs, such as Social Security

per capita income: GDP divided by population

per capita real net public debt: net public debt, deflated by the price level and divided by the population

perfectly inelastic: having an elasticity (or responsiveness) of zero

permanent income: the sustained or average level of income that one expects will be observed over a long period of time

personal consumption expenditures index (PCE): a measure of the dollar cost of purchasing a bundle of goods and services assumed to be representative of the consumption pattern of a typical consumer; one measure of the price level

physical capital: the productive capacity of physical assets, such as buildings

price controls: government rules that limit the prices firms may charge for the goods or services they sell

price level: the average current-year cost, measured relative to the average base-year cost, of a typical basket of goods and services

productivity: output per unit of input

profits: the difference between revenue and cost

progressive tax system: a set of rules that result in the collection of a larger share of income as taxes when income rises

property and contract rights: legal rules governing the use and exchange of property and the enforceable agreements between people or businesses

proportional tax system: a set of rules that result in the collection of an unchanging share of income as income changes

protectionism: economic policy of promoting favored domestic industries through the use of high tariffs and quotas and other trade restrictions to reduce imports

protectionist: any attitude or policy that seeks to prevent foreigners from competing with domestic firms or individuals

public debt: the amount of money owed by a government to its creditors

purchasing power: a measure of the amount of goods and services that can be purchased with a given amount of money

purchasing power parity (PPP): the principle that the relative values of different currencies must reflect their purchasing power in their home countries

quantitative easing (QE): Federal Reserve policy that entails the purchase of various financial assets, conducted in an effort to increase aggregate demand

quota: a limit on the amount of a good that may be imported; generally used to reduce imports so as to protect the economic interests of domestic industries that compete with the imports

real gross domestic product (real GDP): the inflation-adjusted level of new, domestically produced final goods and services

real income: income adjusted for inflation; equivalently, income expressed in terms of goods and services

real interest rate: the premium, in percent per year, that people are willing to pay to have goods sooner rather than later

real per capita income (real GDP per capita): GDP corrected for inflation and divided by the population—a measure of the amount of new domestic production of final goods and services per person

real price: price of a good or service adjusted for inflation; equivalently, the price of a good or service expressed in terms of other goods and services

real purchasing power: the amount of goods and services that can be acquired with an asset whose value is expressed in terms of the monetary unit of account (such as the dollar)

real tax rate: share of GDP controlled by the government

real wages: wages adjusted for changes in the price level

recession: a decline in the level of overall business activity

regressive tax system: a set of rules that result in the collection of a smaller share of income as taxes when income rises

relative prices: prices of goods and services compared to the prices of other goods and services; costs of goods and services measured in terms of other commodities

reparations: payments, in cash or in kind, that must be made from the citizens of one nation to another, often observed as part of the terms of surrender ending a war

required reserves: funds that a commercial bank must lawfully maintain; they may be held in the form of vault cash or deposits at the Fed

reserves: assets held by depository institutions, typically in the form of currency held at the institution or as non-interest-bearing deposits held at the central bank, to meet customers' transaction needs and Fed legal requirements

resources: any items capable of satisfying individuals' desires or preferences or suitable for transformation into such goods

revealed preferences: consumers' tastes as demonstrated by the choices they make

rule of law: the principle that relations between individuals, businesses, and the government are governed by explicit rules that apply to everyone in society

saving: an addition to wealth, conventionally measured as disposable personal income minus consumption

savings: one's stock of wealth at a given moment in time

scarcity: a state of the world in which there are limited resources but unlimited demands, implying that we must make choices among alternatives

share of stock: claim to a specified portion of future net cash flows (or profits) of a corporation

shareholders: owners of shares of stock in a corporation

Social Security: the federal system that transfers income from current workers to current retirees

solvent: describing a financial condition in which the value of one's assets is greater than that of one's liabilities

stagflation: a period of macroeconomic stagnation, combined with inflation

standard of living: a summary measure of the level of per capita material welfare, often measured by per capita real GDP

static economic analysis: a mode of analysis that assumes for simplicity that people do not change their behavior when incentives change

stock: as applied to measurement, an amount measured at a particular moment in time

stockbroker: a middleman who sells shares of stock to individuals

subprime mortgages: mortgages that entail the higher risk of loss for the lender

subsidies: government payments for the production of specific goods, generally intended to raise the profits of the firms producing those goods

supply: the willingness and ability to sell goods

supply and demand: the interaction between willingness and ability to sell, and willingness and ability to buy

systemic risk: hazard that is felt or experienced throughout an entire economy

tariff: a tax levied only on imports; generally used to reduce imports so as to protect the economic interests of domestic industries that compete with the imports

tax bracket: a range of income over which a specific marginal tax rate applies

tax credit: a direct reduction in tax liability, occasioned by a specific set of circumstances and not dependent on the taxpayer's tax bracket

tax evasion: the deliberate failure to pay taxes, usually by making a false report

tax liability: total tax obligation owed by a firm or individual

tax rate: the percentage of a dollar of income that must be paid in taxes

tax rebate: a return of some previously paid taxes

trade barrier: a legal rule imposed by a nation that raises the costs of foreign firms seeking to sell goods in that nation; they include tariffs and quotas

trade deficit: an excess of the value of imports of goods and services over the value of the exports of goods and services

trade surplus: an excess of the value of exports of goods and services over the value of the imports of goods and services

traded goods: goods and services that are exchanged across international borders

Treasury bills: short-term notes of indebtedness of the U.S. government

underground economy: commercial transactions on which taxes and regulations are being avoided

unemployment benefits: regular cash payments made to individuals, contingent on their status as being unemployed

unemployment rate: the number of persons looking and available for work, divided by the labor force

unit of account: the unit in which prices are expressed

unfunded pension liabilities: obligations to make postretirement contractual payment to individuals that are not guaranteed by a sufficient amount of assets as to make the payment virtually certain

unfunded taxpayer liabilities: obligations of taxpayers for which no specific debt instruments have been issued

voucher: a written authorization, exchangeable for cash or services

wealth: the present value of all current and future income

wealth tax: a tax based on a person's net worth

World Trade Organization (WTO): an association of more than 150 nations that helps reduce trade barriers among its members and handles international trade disputes among them

Selected References and Web Links

Chapter 1 Rich Nation, Poor Nation

Easterly, William, and Ross Levine. "Tropics, Germs, and Crops: How Endowments Influence Economic Development." *Journal of Monetary Economics* 50, no. 1 (2003): 3–39.

Mahoney, Paul G. "The Common Law and Economic Growth: Hayek Might Be Right." *Journal of Legal Studies* 30, no. 2 (2001): 503–525.

Rosenberg, Nathan, and L. E. Birdzell Jr. *How the West Grew Rich.* New York: Basic Books, 1987.

www.worldbank.org. Official Web site of the World Bank.

Chapter 2 Outsourcing and Economic Growth

Council of Economic Advisers. *Economic Report of the President.* Washington, D.C.: Government Printing Office, 2004.

Garten, Jeffrey E. "Offshoring: You Ain't Seen Nothin' Yet." *Business Week*, June 21, 2004, p. 28.

Gnuschke, John E., Jeff Wallace, Dennis R. Wilson, and Stephen C. Smith. "Outsourcing Production and Jobs: Costs and Benefits." *Business Perspectives* 16, no. 2 (2004): 12–18.

Irwin, Douglas A. "Free-Trade Worriers." *Wall Street Journal*, August 9, 2004, p. A12.

Reinsdorf, Martin, and Matthew J. Slaughter (eds.). *International Trade in Services and Intangibles in the Era of Globalization.* National Bureau of Economic Research Studies in Income and Wealth, v. 69. Chicago: University of Chicago Press, 2009.

Chapter 3 Poverty, Capitalism, and Growth

www.cia.gov/library/publications/the-world-factbook/index.html. Central Intelligence Agency profiles of countries and territories.

Foundation for Teaching Economics. "Is Capitalism Good for the Poor?" (www.fte.org/capitalism/index.php)

Gwartney, James, Joshua Hall, and Robert Lawson. *Economic Freedom of the World: 2010 Annual Report.* Vancouver, Canada: Fraser Institute, 2010. www.freetheworld.com. Fraser Institute site on economic freedom around the world.

Chapter 4 The Threat to Growth

Edwards, Chris. *Income Tax Rife with Complexity and Inefficiency.* Washington, D.C.: Cato Institute, 2006.

Goolsbee, Austan. "The Impact of the Corporate Income Tax: Evidence from State Organizational Form Data." *Journal of Public Economics* 88, no. 11 (2004): 2283–2299.

Harberger, Arnold C. "Three Basic Postulates for Applied Welfare Economics: An Interpretive Essay." *Journal of Economic Literature* 9, no. 3 (1971): 785–797.

Norton, Rob. "Corporate Taxation." *The Concise Encyclopedia of Economics.* (www.econlib.org/library/Enc/CorporateTaxation.html)

Rakowski, Eric. "Can Wealth Taxes Be Justified?" *Tax Law Review* 53, no. 3 (2000): 3–37.

Chapter 5 Is GDP What We Want?

"Grossly Distorted Picture." *Economist*, March 15, 2008, p. 92.

Steindel, Charles. "Chain Weighting: The New Approach to Measuring GDP." *Current Issues in Economics and Finance* 9, no. 1 (1995): 1–6.

Stevenson, Betsey, and Justin Wolfers. "Economic Growth and Subjective Well-Being: Reassessing the Easterlin Paradox." *Brookings Papers on Economic Activity,* Spring 2008, pp. 1–87. http://www.bea.gov/national/index.htm#gdp. GDP data from U.S. Department of Commerce, Bureau of Economic Analysis.

CHAPTER 6   What's in a Word? Plenty, When It's the "R" Word

Business Cycle Dating Committee. "The NBER's Recession Dating Procedure." National Bureau of Economic Research, 2003. (nber.org/cycles/recessions.html)
Conference Board. "Business Cycle Indicators." (www.globalindicators.org)
Layton, Allan P., and Anirvan Banerji. "What Is a Recession? A Reprise." *Applied Economics* 35, no. 16 (2003): 1789–1797.
www.bea.doc.gov. Web site of the U.S. Department of Commerce's Bureau of Economic Analysis.

CHAPTER 7   The Great Stagflation

Barro, Robert J. "Why This Slow Recovery Ns Like No Recovery." *Wall Street Journal,* June 4, 2012.
Lazear, Edward P. "Whose Fault Is Today's Bad Economy?" *Wall Street Journal,* June 13, 2012.
Congressional Research Service, "Memorandum to Office of the Majority Leader, Representative Eric Cantor." September 14, 2012.
Mulligan, Casey B. "The Safety Net, Work Incentives, and the Economy since 2007." Testimony for the Committee on the Budget, U.S. House of Representatives Hearing on "Strengthening the Safety Net," April 17, 2012.
Walker, Dinah. "Quarterly Update: The U.S. Economic Recovery in Historical Context." Counsel on Foreign Relations, Washington, D.C., November 29, 2012. (http://www.cfr.org/geoeconomics /quarterly-update-us-economic-recovery-historical-context/p25774)
"Welfare Reform as We Knew It." *Wall Street Journal,* September 19, 2012.

CHAPTER 8   The Case of the Disappearing Workers

Benjamin, Daniel K., and Kent G. P. Matthews. *U.S. and U.K. Unemployment between the Wars: A Doleful Story.* London, U.K.: Institute for Economic Affairs, 1992.
Darby, Michael R. "Three-and-a-Half Million U.S. Employees Have Been Mislaid: Or, an Explanation of Unemployment, 1934–1941." *Journal of Political Economy* 84, no. 1 (1976): 1–16.
Jeffrey, Terence P. "8,733,461: Workers on Federal 'Disability' Exceed Population of New York City." *CNSNews.com,* July 2, 2012. (http://cnsnews.com/news/article/8733461-workers-federal-disability-exceed-population-new-york-city)
Wallis, John Joseph, and Daniel K. Benjamin. "Public Relief and Unemployment in the Great Depression." *Journal of Economic History* 41, no. 1 (1981): 97–102.
www.bls.gov. Web site of the U.S. Department of Labor's Bureau of Labor Statistics.
www.socialsecurity.gov/OACT/ProgData/icp.html. Social Security Administration Web site with data on number of recipients and the benefits they receive.

CHAPTER 9   Poverty, Wealth, and Equality

Becker, Gary S., and Richard A. Posner. "How to Make the Poor Poorer." *Wall Street Journal,* January 26, 2007, p. A11.
"Cheap and Cheerful." *Economist,* July 26, 2008, p. 90.
Gabe, Thomas. "Poverty in the United States." Congressional Research Service, Washington, D.C., September 27, 2012.
"Movin' On Up." *Wall Street Journal,* November 13, 2007.
U.S. Department of the Treasury. *Income Mobility in the U.S. from 1996 to 2005.* Washington, D.C.: Government Printing Office, 2007.

CHAPTER 10   Inflation and the Debt Bomb

Alchian, Armen A., and Reuben Kessel. "The Effects of Inflation." *Journal of Political Economy* 70, no. 6 (1962): 521–537.

Cagan, Phillip. "Monetary Dynamics of Hyperinflation." In *Studies in the Quantity Theory of Money*, ed. Milton Friedman. Chicago: University of Chicago Press, 1956.

Keynes, John Maynard. *The Economic Consequences of the Peace*. New York: Harcourt, Brace & Company, 1920.

Rattner, Steven. "The Dangerous Notion That Debt Doesn't Matter." *New York Times*, January 20, 2012.

Spiers, Elizabeth. "The World's Worst Inflation." *Fortune*, August 18, 2008, p. 36.

CHAPTER 11   Is It Real, or Is It Nominal?

Bresnahan, Timothy F., and Robert J. Gordon (eds.). *The Economics of New Goods*. NBER Studies in Income and Wealth no. 58. Chicago: University of Chicago Press, 1997.

Goklany, Indur M., and Jerry Taylor. "A Big Surprise on Gas." *Los Angeles Times*, August 11, 2008.

www.bls.gov. Web site of the Bureau of Labor Statistics, U.S. Department of Labor.

www.eia.doe.gov. Web site of the Energy Information Administration, U.S. Department of Energy.

CHAPTER 12   Who *Really* Pays Taxes?

Congressional Budget Office. "The Distribution of Household Income and Federal Taxes, 2008 and 2009." Congress of the United States: Washington, D.C., July, 2012.

Hollenbeck, Scott, and Maureen Keenan Kahr. "Ninety Years if Individual Income and Tax Statistics, 1916–2005." *Statistics of Income Bulletin*, Winter 2008. (www.irs.gov/uac/IRS-Issues-Winter-2008-Statistics-of-Income-Bulletin)

www.heritage.org/federalbudget/federal-revenue. An array of tax facts, conveniently displayed in pictures.

www.taxpolicycenter.org. Research on taxes, conducted and published by the Brookings Institution.

CHAPTER 13   Are You Stimulated Yet?

Cogan, John F., and John B. Taylor. "The Obama Stimulus Impact? Zero." *Wall Street Journal*, December 9, 2010.

Friedman, Milton, and David Meiselman. "The Relative Stability of Monetary Velocity and the Investment Multiplier in the United States, 1897–1958." In *Commission on Money and Credit: Stabilization Policies*. Englewood Cliffs, NJ: Prentice-Hall, 1963, pp. 165–268.

Merrick, Amy. "Rejecting Stimulus, States Forgo Rail Funds." *Wall Street Journal*, December 10, 2010, p. A6.

Peltzman, Sam. "The Effect of Government Subsidies-In-Kind on Private Expenditures: The Case of Higher Education." *Journal of Political Economy* 81, no. 1 (1973): 1–27.

Saving, Jason. "Can the Nation Stimulate Its Way to Prosperity?" *Economic Letters—Insights from the Federal Reserve Bank of Dallas*. 6, no. 8 (2010): 1–3.

CHAPTER 14   The Fannie Mae, Freddie Mac Flimflam

Applebaum, Binyamin. "Cost of Seizing Fannie and Freddie Surges for Taxpayers." *New York Times*, June 10, 2010.

Berry, Kate. "When Taking on More Bad Loans Seems a Good Idea." *American Banker*, March 15, 2010.

Calomiris, Charles W., and Peter J. Wallison. "Blame Fannie Mae and Congress for the Credit Mess." *Wall Street Journal*, September 23, 2008.

Duhigg, Charles. "Pressured to Take on Risk, Fannie Hit a Tipping Point." *New York Times*, October 5, 2008.

Editorial Staff. "The Biggest Losers." *Wall Street Journal*, January 4, 2010, p. A16.

Editorial Staff. "The Next Fannie Mae." *Wall Street Journal*, August 10, 2009.

Wallison, Peter J. "The Price for Fannie and Freddie Keeps Going Up." *Wall Street Journal*, December 30, 2009, p. A17.

CHAPTER 15 Big Bucks for Bailouts

Crain, Nicole V., and W. Mark Crain. "The Regulation Tax Keeps Growing." *Wall Street Journal,* September 27, 2010, Opinion.

Lerner, Josh. *Boulevard of Broken Dreams.* Princeton, NJ: Princeton University Press, 2009.

Schumpeter, Joseph A. *Capitalism, Socialism, and Democracy.* New York: Harper Perennial Modern Classics, November 2008 [originally published in 1942].

Sherk, James B., and Todd Zywicki. "Obama's United Auto Workers Bailout." *Wall Street Journal.* June 2013, 2012.

Utterback, James M. *Mastering the Dynamics of Innovation.* Cambridge: Harvard Business School Press, 1996.

CHAPTER 16 The Pension Crisis

Brainard, Keith. *Public Fund Survey Summary of Findings for FY2009.* National Association of State Retirement Administrators, October 2010.

Dugan, Ianthe Jeanne. "Facing Budget Gaps, Cities Sell Parking, Airports, Zoo." *Wall Street Journal,* August 23, 2010.

Fitch, Stephan. "Guilt-Edged Pensions." *Forbes,* February 16, 2009, pp. 79–84.

Malanga, Steve. "How States Hide Their Budget Deficits." *Wall Street Journal,* August 23, 2010.

The PEW Center of the States. *The Trillion Dollar Gap: Unfunded State Retirement Systems and the Roads to Reform.* Washington, D.C.: The PEW Charitable Trust, February 2010.

CHAPTER 17 Higher Taxes Are in Your Future

Council of Economic Advisers. *Economic Report of the President.* Washington, D.C.: Government Printing Office, 2013.

The 2012 Annual Report of the Board of Trustees of the Federal Old-Age and Survivors Insurance and Federal Disability Insurance Trust Funds. Washington, D.C.: Government Printing Office, 2012.

U.S. Office of Management and Budget. "Budget of the United States, Fiscal Year 2013." (www. whitehouse.gov/omb/budget)

www.brillig.com/debt_clock. One of many private Web sites that track the U.S. national debt.

www.treasurydirect.gov/NP/BPDLogin?application=np. U.S. Treasury Web site, giving you the current status of the national debt and enabling you to find that status on any working day for the past 20 years.

CHAPTER 18 The Myths of Social Security

Congressional Budget Office. "Social Security: A Primer." September 2001. (www.cbo.gov/showdoc. cfm?index=3213&sequence=0)

Engelhardt, Gary V., and Jonathan Gruber. *Social Security and the Evolution of Elderly Poverty.* NBER Working Paper no. 10466. Boston: National Bureau of Economic Research, 2004.

Oshio, Takashi. *Social Security and Trust Fund Management.* NBER Working Paper no. 10444. Boston: National Bureau of Economic Research, 2004.

www.ssa.gov. Web site of the Social Security Administration.

CHAPTER 19 The Fed and Financial Panics

Friedman, Milton, and Anna J. Schwartz. *A Monetary History of the United States, 1867–1960.* Princeton, NJ: Princeton University Press, 1963.

Goodman, Peter. "Taking a Hard New Look at a Greenspan Legacy." *New York Times,* October 9, 2008.

Norris, Floyd. "Plan B: Flood Banks with Cash." *New York Times,* October 10, 2008.

CHAPTER 20   The Fed Feeding Frenzy

Guha, Krishna, and Tom Braithwaite. "Bernanke Faces Senate Grilling on Confirmation." *Financial Times*, December 2, 2009.

Hilsenrath, Jon. "After Crisis, U.S. Is Set to Rethink Fed's Role." *Wall Street Journal*, May 18, 2009, p. A12.

Hilsenrarth, Jon, and Mark Whitehouse. "Markets Defy Fed's Bond-Buying Push." *Wall Street Journal*, December 9, 2010.

Lang, Jia Lynn, Neil Irwin, and David S. Hizenrath. "Fed Aid in Financial Crisis Went beyond U.S. Banks to Industry, Foreign Firms." *Washington Post*, December 2, 2010.

CHAPTER 21   Deposit Insurance and Financial Markets

Allen, Franklin, and Douglas Gale. "Competition and Financial Stability." *Journal of Money, Credit and Banking* 36, no. 3 (2004): S453–S480.

Bordo, M., H. Rockoff, and A. Redish. "The U.S. Banking System from a Northern Exposure: Stability versus Efficiency." *Journal of Economic History* 54, no. 2 (1994): 325–341.

Diamond, D., and P. Dybvig. "Bank Runs, Deposit Insurance, and Liquidity." *Journal of Political Economy* 91, no. 3 (1983): 401–419.

Friedman, Milton, and Anna J. Schwartz. *A Monetary History of the United States, 1867–1960.* Princeton, NJ: Princeton University Press, 1963.

CHAPTER 22   Phone It In: The Coming Revolution in the Payments System

Diniz, Edwardo, et al., "Mobile Money and Payment: A Literature Review Based on Academic and Practitioner-Oriented Publications" (2001–2011), Proceedings of SIG GlobDev 4th Annual Workshop, Shanghai, China, December 3, 2011.

Helft, Miguel, "The Death of Cash," *Fortune*, July 23, 2012, p. 118ff.

Vander Weyer, Martin, "Does PayTag Mean the End of Cash in Your Pocket?" *The Telegraph*, Saturday, October 20, 2012.

CHAPTER 23   The Value of the Dollar

Clark, Peter, et al. *Exchange Rates and Economic Fundamentals*. IMF Occasional Paper no. 115. Washington, D.C.: International Monetary Fund, 1994.

finance.yahoo.com/currency-converter?u. One of many private currency converters available online.

Grant, James. "Is the Medicine Worse than the Illness?" *Wall Street Journal*, December 20, 2008.

www.exchange-rates.org. One of many private currency converters available online.

CHAPTER 24   Is The Eurozone Zoning Out?

Charlemagne, "SimEurope: Some Fantasies for the Future of Europe May Cause More Problems than They Resolve," *The Economist*, September 22, 2012, p. 64.

Fidler, Stephen, "Spanish Bailout Is No Fix for Italy's Woes," *Wall Street Journal Europe*, October 5–7, 2012, p. 4.

Gianviti, Francois, et al., "A European Mechanism for Sovereign Debt Crisis Resolution: A Proposal," *Bruegel Blueprint Series*, vol. X, 2010.

CHAPTER 25   The Global Power of the Big Mac

Ashenfelter, Orley, and Stepan Jurajda, "Comparing Real Wages," NBER Working Paper No. 18006. (www.nber.org/papers/w18006, April, 2012)

Ashenfelter, Orley, and Stepan Jurajda, "Cross-Country Comparisons of Wage Rates: The McWage Index," Industrial Relations Section, Princeton University, Princeton, NJ, August 2009.

Clementi, Fabio, et al., "A Big Mac Test of Price Dynamics and Dispersion of Across Euro Area," *Economic Bulletin* 30, no. 3, August (2010): 2037–2053.

CHAPTER 26   The Opposition to Globalization

Frankel, J. A., and D. Romer. "Does Trade Cause Growth?" *American Economic Review* 89, no. 3 (1999): 379–399.

"Indian Call Center Lands in Ohio." *Fortune*, August 6, 2007, p. 23.

Makki, Shiva S., and Agapi Somwaru. "Impact of Foreign Direct Investment and Trade on Economic Growth: Evidence from Developing Countries." *American Journal of Agricultural Economics* 86, no. 3 (2004): 795–801.

CHAPTER 27   The $750,000 Job

Congressional Budget Office. "The Pros and Cons of Pursuing Free-Trade Agreements." July 2003. (www.cbo.gov/showdoc.cfm?index=4458&sequence=0)

Greider, William. "A New Giant Sucking Sound: China Is Taking away Mexico's Jobs as Globalization Enters a Fateful New Stage." *Nation*, December 31, 2001, p. 22.

"Stolen Jobs? Offshoring." *Economist*, December 13, 2003, p. 15.

INDEX